Japan's
Hidden Hot Springs

SEN1, p 181
FUKUOHI, p. 113

Koshinetsu Region – Nagano Prefect.
train to Matsumoto

ROBERT NEFF

Japan's
Hidden Hot Springs

CHARLES E. TUTTLE COMPANY
Rutland, Vermont & Tokyo, Japan

Brush illustrations by Shigeko Nakayama

Published by the Charles E. Tuttle Company, Inc.
of Rutland, Vermont & Tokyo, Japan
with editorial offices at
2-6 Suido 1-chome, Bunkyo-ku, Tokyo 112

LCC Card No. 93-61750
ISBN 0-8048-1949-1

First edition, 1995

Printed in Japan

♨ **Contents** ♨

A MAP for each region appears on the first page of the
section devoted to that region.
PHOTOGRAPHS of representative hot springs are on pages
81–88.

♨ *Acknowledgments* ♨

Nothing enhances the *onsen* experience more than good companionship. For that I've been richly blessed. First comes my wife, Fumiko Sekizawa, whose capacity for enjoying hot springs may even exceed my own. Together we explored many of the places featured in this guide. From the early days we were often accompanied by one or more of a merry band of dedicated epicures and great pals—Makoto (Tama-chan) and Keiko Endo, Nobuko Kato and Hideko Miyazaki. We've also shared multiple *onsen* revelries over the years with our good friends Phillipe Huber and Miho Shigematsu, Mark Cote, Urban Lehner and Nancy Leonard, Peter and Yu-Ling Wolff, Mark Schreiber, and Joe and Megumi McFatridge. To all of them, thanks for the memories and the trips to come.

For inspiration, encouragement and invaluable tips I salute Robin Berrington, the Nihon Hito o Mamorukai, David Chapman, and Fuyuto Noguchi's classic *Rotenburo Gaido* (Kankando Shuppansha, 1981).

Lastly, for the photos that grace these pages, I thank the Gendai Ryoko Kenkyusho.

♨ *Introduction* ♨

What ever happened to the "real" Japan? It's a question heard all too often from newcomers and long-time foreign residents alike in a country that's rapidly yielded to rampant concrete, vinyl, vending machines, and loudspeakers. Is Japan's once-vaunted serenity, subtlety, and affinity for the sublime gone forever? Unfortunately, yes, for the most part. But there are a few scattered repositories of unspoiled Japan that refuse to die. Among them are the magical hidden hot springs that usually escape the attention of foreigners searching for traditional Japan.

All too many *onsen*, or hot springs, have become garish monuments of tackiness, to be sure. Unfortunately, it is these towns—including Atami, Beppu, Kusatsu, Noboribetsu, and Kinugawa—that most foreigners know. They either aren't aware of, or fear seeking out, the more isolated and charming alternatives. Many wind up staying at relatively mundane places when practically next door a far more salubrious alternative awaits. At the risk of speeding the ruination of these rare remaining spots, this book attempts to guide you to places that evoke the spirit and ambiance of years gone by. No one to my knowledge has offered a selective, English-language guide to specific hot-spring inns that represent the height of the *onsen* experience.

This book's main entries represent the best of the literally hundreds of *onsen* inns I've visited over the years. They're the rough, modest equivalent of three Michelin stars, which Michelin defines as worth a journey. The accompanying sub-entries, separated from the main ones by a 〰 symbol, are worth a detour, or two stars. My selections are completely independent. I have received no form of consideration from any organization nor any of the featured inns; none of them was aware I was preparing a guidebook. I personally visited each of them, almost always had a bath, and usually spent a night or two (or three).

The spas of the Roman Empire—England's Bath and Italy's Montecatini Terme come to mind—were developed in earlier times. But there's probably no culture that's conducted as extensive a love affair with hot springs as Japan. This volcanic archipelago is dotted with literally thousands of mineral springs, around 2,300 of which boast at least one inn. Unlike their contemporary Western counterparts, these *onsen* are used less for therapeutic purposes than for recreation. To be sure, each spring claims certain curative powers. But the premium is on the bucolic, not the clinical. *Onsen* are to Baden-Baden as Big Sur is to the Mayo Clinic.

My own experience with *onsen* dates back to 1960, when, as a thirteen-year-old, I moved to Japan from Missouri with my missionary parents. Soon after arriving, we and a couple of other American families took a holiday at what was then one of Asia's premier resort hotels: Kowakien in Hakone. I was fully unprepared for the mixed bathing we encountered there. I'll never forget trying to run for cover after spotting several naked middle-aged Japanese women in the changing room. It took my father's missionary-honed persuasiveness to entice me into the bath. My other significant memory is of how hot it was. For the rest of our five-year stay I had occasion to visit other hot springs. And during the year I spent in Japan after college, I sampled still more.

But my real infatuation with *onsen* began in 1979, when I returned for the third time, as a correspondent for *Business Week*. Jarred by the incredible modernization that had occurred during the nineteen years since my first arrival, I began seeking out places that nurtured the kind of traditional, natural ambiance I remembered from the early sixties. It didn't take long to discover that certain *onsen* did. Since then, I've taken temporary refuge from Tokyo at dozens of springs throughout the country, always seeking out the hidden ones that preserve the flavor of bygone days.

You should know my prejudices: I strongly favor single-inn *onsen*, which helps assure the tranquil, unspoiled milieu that a proper hot-spring experience requires. With some exceptions, I prefer a place with an outdoor bath. Ideally, the inn should be off the road, at a dead end or a short hike in, and conserve a traditional motif. Not all of the places I've chosen completely meet these criteria but most come close. I also don't want to excessively strain myself getting to a spring: My limit is about thirty minutes of walking. Hidden *onsen* requiring a long hike up a trail tend to be barracks-like quarters aimed at serious backpackers as opposed to seekers of rest and relaxation. For travelers relying on public transportation, the walk from the nearest stop might be more than thirty minutes to some of the featured inns. Bus routes should be confirmed in advance. But in most cases the inn will pick you up. And I'm assuming that many readers will employ their own vehicles, rental cars, taxis, or hitchhiking to get as close as possible.

One word of caution: The Japanese have a penchant for supplanting charming wooden structures with concrete eyesores that are totally out of touch with the environment. Unfortunately, more than a few *onsen* have fallen prey to this proclivity and the trend is accelerating. Among the worst offenders are Kaniyu in Tochigi's wilderness Oku-Kinugawa Onsen enclave, remote Tomuraushi in Hokkaido, and funky Yunoyama in Hiroshima. Until recently, these quaint places were among Japan's most evocative hidden *onsen*. Now they've been scarred or replaced by concrete monstrosities. Elsewhere, once-charming *onsen* have been blighted by the construction of a new highway or dam within easy sight. Bottom line: There's a chance that the atmosphere of some of the places described herein has egregiously changed since my last visit. So you should ask, when seeking a reservation, whether the inn or its surroundings have been significantly revamped within the past few years, and if so, how.

At the same time, an inn needn't be ancient, decrepit, and in the middle of nowhere to make this guide. Few are, in fact. A number are luxurious, virtually all are well-kept, and most are within relatively easy striking distance. Some are even in small *onsen* villages. Many of my choices have been painstakingly modernized, or even completely rebuilt, with superb character. Others have been lovingly maintained for decades.

When describing baths, I'm usually referring to the men's bath unless I specify otherwise. Which reminds me: several friends who knew I was writing this book asked whether I would specify which inns still have mixed bathing, since they like to bathe with loved ones of the opposite sex. I have therefore prepared a list, on page 169, of the places in this guide that offered *kon'yoku* as of early 1994. But as I mention in Appendix 1 (p. 163), it's often easy to "integrate" baths that are formally segregated. In each entry I'm always sure to mention whether there's a *rotenburo* (outdoor bath) or not. No mention, no *rotenburo*.

There are better times than others for visiting *onsen*. Winter is best, since the hot water feels finest against the cold air and the snowscapes are so ethereal. What could be more sublime than sitting in a mountain hot tub at night, sipping saké and conversing with your close ones while gazing at the stars through snow-clad branches? Ideally, a bubbling brook is coursing through the snow just next to the bath. Great for a Scandinavian-style plunge if your heart can take it. The next-best season is autumn, followed by spring and summer. Avoid weekends if possible, although that's when I usually go for lack of other opportunities. And try to take friends. You'll get a better room and price as a party of four (or more) and have more fun as well.

This guide is skewed toward northeastern Honshu (Tohoku) and the southern island of Kyushu, since that's where geology dictates most springs are to be found. But I lean toward the former for its more traditional ways and relative lack of commercialization. I've also tried hard to include as many inns as possible that are within easy reach of Tokyo, since that's from where most readers will be heading. For Hokkaido, more recently developed than other regions, I've had to apply a somewhat different set of standards. Since few inns there resonate with a traditional ambiance, I looked for those with pristine natural surroundings, rustic atmosphere, and good baths. Shikoku didn't rate entry in this guide at all because, as most *onsen* experts will agree, it lacks alluring springs.

Like virtually all of Shikoku's so-called *onsen*, some on the other three main islands are actually *kosen*, or cool mineral-springs. They generally contain at least as many of the reportedly curative properties of true *onsen* but must be artificially heated. Most call themselves *onsen* and are usually recognized as such. With rare exception I find them estimable and unworthy of discrimination.

Regarding prices, I steer clear of inns that run over 20,000 yen a night per person. Higher-priced *onsen* tend to be in overly developed areas, anyway. Each entry in this book is assigned a basic-price category as of 1994: A—8,000 yen or less per person; B —12,000 or under; C—up to 16,000 yen; D—no more than 20,000 yen. These prices incorporate *hoshiryo*, or service charges, when applicable, but do not include consumption and *onsen* taxes. Given Japan's minimal inflation, prices aren't likely to change much for awhile. Many inns offer a wide range of tariffs, reflecting the desirability of the room, the choice of food, the number of guests per room, and the season or day of the week. There's often a Saturday-night premium. During winter, some rustic inns impose a heating charge of about 500 yen a head.

If you live in Japan, join the Nihon no Hito o Mamoru Kai, or Association to Protect Japan's Hidden Springs, and buy its small guidebook, *Nihon no Hito*. Many of the one hundred affiliated establishments are attuned to the values of this guide. Best of all, each can supply you with a pamphlet that you can get stamped at each member location where you stay. Once you've collected ten stamps you can spend one weeknight free of charge at any participating inn. The address is: c/o Asahi Ryoko Kai, 2 Kanda Iwamoto-cho, Chiyoda-ku, Tokyo 101. Phone: (03) 3252-5321.

In accordance with Japanese usage, I have not used plurals in rendering Japanese words. So when referring to multiple *onsen* or *rotenburo*, for example, I have not added a plural "s." At the beginning of each section, you'll find a map indicating the general location of each of the featured spas. At the back of the book you'll find a glossary of the language you'll encounter as well as the Japanese terms used in this guide. I've also included an appendix that provides pointers on everything from making a reservation and checking in to etiquette in the bath.

Enjoy!

The
Hidden Hot Springs

Daisetsu Kōgen Onsen

One of only two Hokkaido inns I've chosen as main entries, Daisetsu Kogen Sanso ranks among the friendliest, best-managed *onsen* in Japan. It's also refreshingly remote, despite its relative proximity to the ruinously developed Sounkyo Gorge tourist mecca. At the end of a minimally maintained but easily driveable ten-kilometer mountain track in the Daisetsuzan National Park, this large wooden lodge, located 1,350 meters above sea level, is Hokkaido's highest hot spring. It's the jumping-off point for several trails, the most popular and shortest of which is a three-hour wander among dozens of high-mountain marshes and ponds. In late June the snow was still so deep that we had to turn back after an hour.

Presumably because I'm a foreigner, the two of us were given by far the best room in the inn—"Komagusa"—for the same rock-bottom price as that charged for considerably inferior quarters. Beautifully appointed (for such a rustic lodge) "Komagusa" is actually a suite comprising eighteen tatami mats. Our maid proudly told us this is where the Emperor Showa stayed in 1968. (I didn't have the courage to ask whether he used the communal toilets, as everyone now must). So try to reserve Komagusa. If it's not available, ask for neighboring "Togazakura" or "Kokemomo." The other eleven rooms are pedestrian.

This place unfortunately lacks a *rotenburo*. But the straightforward indoor baths offer up terrific water. Cobalt-blue and pleasantly redolent of minerals, at forty-two degrees centigrade they're almost perfect. For the first time in my experience, while I was soaking the bath-master entered with a thermometer to check the water temperature. I told him it was just right and he seemed to agree. Beyond comfort, the baths were generally deserted despite a nearly full house.

In a location this remote, one usually doesn't expect much from the cuisine. We were gratified to find otherwise. The inn's hallmark duck stew is hearty and delicious. *Chawanmushi* doesn't come much better and local mountain vegetables are presented in several mouth-watering ways. All this and more is served warm on heavy wooden tables in a commodious, wood-beamed dining room replete with a massive stone-clad hearth and open kitchen. Having tipped our maid at the outset, we received attentive service at both meals.

Expecting mild weather in late June, I arrived without anything warm to wear against the surprisingly cold and snowy elements. Not to worry. As we set out on our hike the solicitous manager eagerly found a jacket and boots for me. The maid came running after us with towels to use as mufflers. Returning well after checkout time, we were graciously invited to bathe free of charge.

> **Daisetsu Kōgen Sansō**
> Daisetsu Kogen, Sounkyo, Kamikawa-cho, Kamikawa-gun,
>   Hokkaido 078-17
> PHONE: 01658-5-3818   PRICE: B
> TRANSPORTATION: From Kamikawa Station on the Ishikita Line, the
>   bus to Sounkyo Onsen takes 35 minutes. Then taxi
>   for 40 minutes.
>   BY CAR: From Route 39 south of Sounkyo, turn at the sign
>   near Kogen Ohashi and you're 10 kilometers away.

✳ ✳ ✳

Pirika Onsen

As newly developed *onsen* go, Yama no Ie has to be one of the quaintest and most satisfying. An ancient spring used by the Ainu, whose term *pirika* means "beautiful river," this remote spa lay derelict for decades until the distant town of Imakane that encompasses Pirika decided to restore it a few years ago. In typical Hokkaido fashion, the town fathers opted against traditional Japanese aesthetics in favor of a cozy cabin configuration. They chose wisely. Log-built Yama no Ie and its detached bathhouse of matching motif perfectly suit the arboreal surroundings.

Huddled into a captivating glade trisected by two streams at the end of a long, narrow road, Yama no Ie's appeal is less to seekers of ancient Japan than to nature lovers. There's not a phone- or power-line in sight. Cars are kept well away. Vegetation abounds.

The naturalist aspect was driven home to me one morning while soaking alone near the edge of the rocky *rotenburo*. Feeling a strange, fleeting sensation on my back, I wheeled around to discover that a meter-long rat snake had just slithered across my shoulders, apparently mistaking them for a rock. Fortunately, rat snakes (*aodaisho*) are harmless to humans.

The snake's presence was testimony to Pirika's comfortingly lukewarm water. Too tepid for some tastes, perhaps, but great for long, luxurious soaks. Smack beside the mixed-bathing *rotenburo* is the rustic bathhouse, which contains segregated, soothing pools beneath a high ceiling supported by enormous log beams. No concrete or tile here. The nighttime lighting is ethereal.

The inn, paneled with the aromatic wood of *hinoki*, a cypresslike tree, is simplicity itself. Toilets and washroom are shared and there are only five guest rooms, all on the second floor. There's no TV, no furniture, and no phones in the rooms. You roll out your own futon. But the quarters are bright, airy, and quiet, with verdant views. Ask for a corner room. There's also the option of staying in one of two nearby cottages. Romantic indeed, but they contain no facilities.

Yama no Ie's staff consists of one middle-aged couple. Mr. Ota, a former chef, cooks up a storm given the isolated circumstances. Our dinner, served in the narrow first-floor dining area, comprised a delicious tempura of *yamame* river fish, mountain vegetables as delectably prepared as any we've tasted, *himemasu sashimi*, squid that would do any sushi shop proud, and assorted side dishes of equal quality.

Out in the sprawling yard, near one of the rivers, lies a pleasant barbecue area. If you're around for lunch, Ota-san will sell you a platter of meat and even provide charcoal.

For those wanting to get away from it all, this is bliss.

Yama no Ie
Pirika, Imakane-cho, Setana-gun, Hokkaido
PHONE (representative): 01378-3-7111   PRICE: A
TRANSPORTATION: From Oshamanbe Station on the Hakodate Line, a taxi takes 40 minutes.
BY CAR: From Kunnui on Route 5 below Oshamanbe, take Route 230 for 11.5 kilometers to Pirika Lake. Turn right and follow the signs for about 8 kilometers.

〰

Horoka
Renowned for its curative waters, isolated Horoka is an interesting diversion. Perched above a glade about one kilometer in from a main wilderness road, the verdant enclave of three small, scattered inns offers up a potpourri of baths. Your best lodging bet is Horoka Onsen Ryokan, a gray, two-storied wooden structure with pedestrian men's and women's baths and a mixed *rotenburo*. By far the more interesting bathing is at the neighboring (but tacky) Yumotokan Shika-no-Tani. The funky *kon'yoku* bathhouse features four pools of noticeably differing waters— natrium, calcium, iron, and sulfur. Out back lies a small but comfy *rotenburo* with leafy views. Stroll over from your quarters and pay 400 yen for access. The third inn is dedicated to self-cooking (*jisuibu*) and boasts a quaint *rotenburo* near the stream.

Horoka Onsen Ryokan

Kamishihoro-machi, Horoka Bangaichi, Hokkaido
PHONE: 01564-4-2167   PRICE: A
TRANSPORTATION: From Obihiro on the Nemuro Line, take the bus to Nukadaira Onsen for 90 minutes. Change to the "taxi-bus" bound for Kamishihoro and ride for 20 minutes to Horoka Onsen Iriguchi. Then walk about 25 minutes.

Metō Onsen

This is a restful, out-of-the-way spring that's worth a detour. Without your own wheels it's an hour's walk from the nearest bus stop. But you can drive or hitchhike to the front door via pastoral back roads. As in most Hokkaido *onsen* the interior and exterior lack charm. But the inn is bright and clean and is in a gem of a setting. A couple of hundred meters off the gravel road, Meto rests beside a soothing stream in a verdant glen. Once settled into your spacious, toilet-equipped room, head straight for the pleasant *rotenburo*. The water is clear, the temperature perfect, and the rocky design pleasingly capacious. The food here is decent and the welcome friendly. We were sorry to leave.

Metō Onsen

2979 Meto, Ashoro-machi, Ashoro-gun, Hokkaido
PHONE: 01562-6-2119   PRICE: B
TRANSPORTATION: From Ashoro Station on the Furusato Ginga Line, take the bus bound for Obihiro for about 25 minutes to Meto. Or from Obihiro Station on the Nemuro Line, take the bus bound for Ashoro for about 90 minutes to Meto. The inn can arrange to pick you up there.

Yamada Onsen

From the outside, you'd give this place an immediate pass. But Yamada gets my reserved vote for its memorable food, down-home service, and surrounding countryside. Several kilometers from the nearest settlement at Shikaribetsu Lake but smack-dab against the mountain road, lonely Yamada looks totally charmless from the outside. Our drab, tiny room and the unexceptional bath didn't immediately improve our spirits. But this place gradually grew on us. For the price, the food is unmatched in our experience. Never have I devoured such a tender, succulent sauté of venison. Add in the local lake fish served in two styles, the superb raw prawns, exceptional salmon sushi, and delectable noodles and you've got a meal to remember. Breakfast was the best we had in Hokkaido. What's more, the disarming manager let us use his washing machine. Despite its roadside setting, Yamada is tranquil. In the large backyard compound we watched a family of wandering deer and on the road to Nukadaira Onsen we encountered perhaps a dozen wild foxes.

Yamada Onsen Hotel Fukuhara
Shikaribetsu-ko, Shikaoi-machi, Kawahigashi-gun, Hokkaido
PHONE: 01566-7-2302   PRICE: A
TRANSPORTATION: From Obihiro on the Nemuro Line, take the bus bound for Nukadaira Onsen for 90 minutes. Taxi for 25 minutes. Closed in winter.

Tokachidake Onsen

Inns don't come much more decrepit than this and the food is marginal. But Ryounkaku survives by offering up one of Japan's most breath-taking *rotenburo* views at a trailhead into some of Hokkaido's best backpacking country. Perched above a plunging river gorge at the end of a long, steep mountain road from trendy Furano, Ryounkaku is a crumbling hikers' lodge built years ago with materials carried in by horseback. Today the indoor baths are dank and the rooms almost cell-like. But if you can spend most of your time in the murky water of the mixed-bathing *rotenburo* you'll come away satisfied. The scenery is simply resplendent. Just a few kilometers down the road toward Shirogane

Onsen, stop at the secluded, town-managed Fukiage *rotenburo*. There's no inn but the nicely arranged clear pools are heavenly. Best of all, they are free.

> **Ryōunkaku**
> Kami-Furano-cho, Sorachi-gun, Hokkaido 071-05
> PHONE: 0167-45-2572   PRICE: B
> TRANSPORTATION: The bus to Tokachidake Onsen takes 45 minutes from Kami-Furano Station on the Furano Line.

Sakurano Onsen

Ginkonyu is the best-known hidden spring in these parts and isn't a bad place to stay. But I prefer the cozier Kumaneso (Lodge of the Sleeping Bear). The motif is that of a modern hunting lodge. Well off a deserted road and next to the rushing Nodaoi River, tranquillity is assured. Another draw is value for money. For just 7400 yen each, the two of us enjoyed a sparkling, traditionally decorated twelve-tatami-mat room and terrific food. Dinner included a delicious, lightly deep-fried stuffed crab, a tantalizing vegetable sauté, broiled *yamame* river fish, and more. Best of all, everything was freshly cooked and warm. The simple but tasteful baths offer hot, murky-brown water of high quality. Ask for one of the four large rooms facing the river. Beware: like many Hokkaido *onsen*, Kumaneso doesn't provide towels.

> **Kumanesō**
> Yakumo-cho, Yamakoshi-gun, Hokkaido
> PHONE: 01376-6-2564   PRICE: A
> TRANSPORTATION: From Noda Oi or Yakumo stations on the Hakodate Line, Kumaneso will fetch you in a van.

Tashiro Motoyu Onsen

To visit Tashiro Motoyu Onsen is to travel back to the Japan of Townsend Harris and Lafcadio Hearn. Forget that you're technically within the bounds of Aomori City. Here you'll find no concessions to modern times: no electricity or phone, no cars, no concrete. This is the *onsen* connoisseur's *onsen*; my vision of the quintessential hidden spring; the magic of a Japan untouched.

By the time you negotiate the rocky kilometer-long road from the isolated bus stop to the clearing for cars and start descending the steep ten-minute path to Yamada-kan, you suspect you're penetrating a separate reality. Once you cross the low swinging bridge over the narrow Komagomi River, you know it for sure. Arriving at the bottom of the misty, beech-shrouded hollow, you suddenly espy an inviting *rotenburo* to the right. Beyond is a roofed outdoor pool fast by a rustic wooden bathhouse with steam streaming from its cupola. Nestled beyond, weathered and wooden Yamada-kan beckons. There's nothing else in sight but Mother Nature.

At the *genkan* you'll be greeted by the kimono-clad octogenarian proprietress, Mrs. Yamada. So thick is her local accent that even native Tokyoites only get about half of what she's saying. No problem. Tell her your name and she'll helpfully guide you to your room. It will be tiny and crude, defined mainly by sliding *fusuma* doors. What else to do but don your *yukata* robe (bring your own, along with a towel) and head for the bath!

Unlike most *onsen* inns, Yamada-kan contains no bath within its walls. Instead, slip into wooden sandals and shuffle over to the bathhouse. There you'll find separate changing rooms for men and women. But the two-tub bath itself is integrated; Tashiro

Motoyu is one of the rare *onsen* that don't bother accommodating separate sexes in any of its baths. This suits most of the guests just fine. With all inhibitions down, quiet conversation with fellow bathers comes easy.

Like the inn, the high-ceilinged bathhouse is eerily lit at night with oil lamps. Truly ethereal. From there you can walk naked to the adjoining roofed pool with lukewarm water and on to the hotter main *rotenburo*. Off to the right is a lean-to offering a *takiyu*, or waterfall bath, with water streaming from three separate pipes: the original shower massage. Just beyond is a humble shack with yet another rustic tub of murky water.

Lacking electricity and modern cooking facilities, Yamada-kan recently stopped serving food and now asks guests to bring their own. There is a simple kitchen where you can warm things up. Mrs. Yamada says she's deliberately avoided installing a generator so as to preserve the traditional atmosphere. This makes her one of a nearly extinct breed, so take advantage of it while you can.

Yamada-kan
1-13-7 Fukazawa, Komagomi, Aomori-shi, Aomori-ken
Closed in winter.
PHONE: 0177-66-0506 (representative)   PRICE: A
TRANSPORTATION: Take the bus from Aomori Station bound for Hakkodo Eight Line for 55 minutes. Get off at Gotogocho Ozomae and walk for 30 minutes.
BY CAR: From Route 4 in central Aomori City, take the local road heading south and follow the signs for "Tashirotai" for about 20 kilometers. Watch for a crude sign on the left.

✳   ✳   ✳

Aoni Onsen

Could this be the hidden *onsen* of the future? If so, there's reason to be hopeful. Until 1982, Aoni Onsen epitomized the primitive mountain spring. From the nearest road it was more than a two-hour hike into a deep, secluded valley where one was greeted by a lonely, thatch-roofed inn with no electricity. Certain literati adopted it as their own special sanctuary. Then, armed with a magnificent vision, owner Eiji Sawada embarked on a bold expansion scheme. However, unlike most of his counterparts at other *onsen*, he eschewed concrete and opted to build several new wooden structures in a wonderfully traditional mode. Today, Aoni stands as rare testimony that *onsen* inns can be modernized with magnificent grace.

If you look hard enough you'll discover that Aoni now has electricity. But there's not a light fixture in the place. It remains as one of no more than a half-dozen inns illuminated solely by oil lamps. The power is strictly for refrigeration and anti-fire sensors. The new buildings are stylishly appointed in traditional woods, sliding shoji doors, and log beams. Inside the main building, you'll find two pristine cypress baths of supreme elegance. The large, boulder-strewn, roofed *rotenburo* measures up to almost any in Japan, while the separate bathhouse contains an utterly transparent pool floored with large, consummately smooth black stones. All of this is set in a broad, tastefully landscaped glade festooned with a natural waterfall and various attractive outbuildings, including the thatched original structure. No inn offers so many desirable attractions for such a modest tariff.

Our room, in a quiet building to the rear of the main inn, was sparklingly spare but comfortingly traditional. If those two characteristics seem dissonant, trust me. We had a pleasant garden view and were completely undisturbed.

The only thing keeping Aoni from the top of my rankings is the commercialism that flickers around the edges. A new seven-kilometer road from the highway now gives way to the occasional tour bus. The coffee shop off the small lobby is traditionally appointed but slightly kitsch. The staff tends toward student part-timers. Meals in the capacious, tatami-floored dining room are mass-produced affairs. Overall, the putative traditionalism smacks slightly of the artificial.

Still, Aoni should captivate all but the absolute purist. Here you'll get much of the lamp-lit magic of a Tashiro Motoyu with many more amenities and creature comforts.

Aoni Onsen Ryokan
117 Takinoue Aonisawa, Okiura, Kuroishi-shi, Aomori-ken
PHONE: 0172-54-8588   PRICE: B
TRANSPORTATION: Arrange with the inn for the twice-daily bus from Kuroishi Station on the Konan Line, but it's much easier by rental car, perhaps from Aomori Station.
BY CAR: Take Route 102 southeast toward Towadako from Kuroishi for about 16 kilometers. Turn left just before Aoni-bashi and drive 7 kilometers.

✳ ✳ ✳

Nurukawa Onsen

Not nearly as spectacular as Aoni Onsen less than twenty kilometers up the road, nurturing Nurukawa still has a special place in my heart. Nestled into a tree-shrouded rise just off quiet Highway 102 a few kilometers below the north shore of Lake Towada, this verdant single-inn spring offers a cozier class of comfort than resplendent Aoni.

Park in the lot on the far side of the road and cross the swinging bridge over the narrow Hiyako River. Climb the small incline up to the broad *genkan* and you'll be warmly greeted in sincere, homey style. Once you've entered, you'll notice the comfy dining room on the right, though you'll be given the option of eating in your quarters if you prefer.

On the way to your room you may be put off by the tacky hallways. A peek into the relatively charmless indoor baths along the way may also disappoint. But much better things are in store. Assuming you've reserved the best room in the house—"Bokke"—

you can't help but be happy. At the innermost reaches of the inn, it's quiet and private. Simply but soothingly decorated, "Bokke" comprises ten tatami mats plus an entryway, a carpeted sitting area next to broad windows facing a thick glen of beech and maples, and a Western-style toilet. For two people paying just 13,000 yen each in late 1993, it felt like a heavenly bargain, especially considering the dinner that was to come.

We opted, correctly, to eat in the lovely dining area just off the *genkan*. There, sitting on chairs at a table, we were treated to a sumptuous repast of trout *sashimi*, hot tempura, broiled eel, rockfish steamed in a leaf with *miso*, a delectable stew, and other delights. All in a serene, softly lit space.

For bathing, forget the forgettable indoor baths and head straight for the newly constructed, mixed-bathing *rotenburo*. It's wonderful. Designed and built by members of Nurukawa Sanso's staff in memory of a noteworthy nineteenth-century local who'd built his own *rotenburo*, this is one of the best modern renditions I've encountered. The stairway and changing rooms are log-hewn and rustic. The bath itself is roomy, floored with slate and circumscribed by dense woods. The water is clear, odorless, and perfectly hot. Highway 102 is just a stone's throw away, but the river's sound and the thick foliage disguise it well.

If you're lucky enough to be visiting in autumn, drive a few kilometers north to the left-hand turnoff at the southern tip of Lake Niji. About twenty minutes after entering the prefectural road heading toward Owani-cho, you'll descend into some of the most beautiful apple country Aomori has to offer. We stopped at one particularly picturesque orchard along the way in a village called Komaki and arranged for the keeper to send fresh apples to several friends of ours in Tokyo.

Nurukawa Sansō
Nurukawa, Hiraka-machi, Minami-Tsugaru-gun, Aomori-ken
PHONE: 0172-55-2314   PRICE: B, C
TRANSPORTATION: From Kuroishi Station on the Konan Line, take the

bus to Towadako Konoguchi for 65 minutes. Alight at Nurukawa Sanso-mae.

BY CAR: It's about 5 kilometers northwest of Lake Towada on Route 102.

Tsuta Onsen

One of my great regrets is never having stayed at this legendary inn. Despite passing it several times over the years, scheduling always seemed to allow only a daytime dip. It would almost certainly be a main entry if I'd had the chance to spend a night. Among Tohoku's most prized yet remote *onsen*, Tsuta boasts many delights. Topping the list are its magnificently evocative baths. All three—one for women, two for men—are beamed with massive logs and completely clad in ancient wood. Clear, odorless spring water bubbles up between cracks in the tubs' planked bottoms. The huge main building likewise resonates antiquity. A newer annex is tasteful and essentially hidden and several nature trails lead away from the inn, replete with birds and ponds. Tsuta is slightly marred by a huge parking lot, souvenir shop, and restaurant wing. But surrounded as it is by a dense beech forest on a lush mountain road, Tsuta is tranquil and inviting. Nearby Oirase Gorge is delightful to walk through.

Tsuta Onsen Ryokan
Towadako-machi, Kamikita-gun, Aomori-ken
PHONE: 0176-74-2311   PRICE: C, D
TRANSPORTATION: From Aomori Station, take the bus for Towadako for 2 hours and 20 minutes. (Bus doesn't run in winter.)

Matsukawa Onsen

Physically disappointing on the surface, this inn takes a bit of time to appreciate. On top of the presence of an ugly parking lot and a ramshackle, charmless edifice come rooms of the most utilitarian nature. Yet all this serves to disguise one of the better *onsen* experiences, as the difficulty in getting a room at Shofuso testifies.

First comes the setting. Isolated Matsukawa Onsen lies at the end of a narrow mountain road and comprises three widely spaced inns essentially invisible from one another, thanks mainly to the rough topography and thick foliage. The quiet little enclave makes for a memorably romantic evening stroll in your *yukata* robe and *geta* sandals. Doing so, you'll note that the other two inns aren't as rustic. And they couldn't be any more welcoming than Shofuso, where we were greeted disarmingly. No one treated me like an errant Westerner.

What distinguishes Shofuso is its two mixed-bathing *rotenburo*. The commodious main one, at the far end of the inn, sits majestically above the river from which this spring derives its name. The deeply translucent, sulfur-infused water in this bath is hot. All the better for intermittently crawling out to cool off in the brisk Iwate air and to gaze at the stream and the bucolic surroundings. From this vantage point you'll espy the swinging bridge crossing the river to Shofuso's treasure, the cave-like rock bath tucked into the far bank.

The water in this half-open, natural pool is clear as it comes from a different spring than the main *rotenburo*. It's also much cozier but can easily handle a half-dozen people at a time. On our first dip we shared it comfortably with a mother and her adolescent son and daughter. This would have to rank as one of the paragons of *rotenburo* bathing.

Less than thirty minutes back down the road from Matsukawa Onsen is the entrance to one of Japan's most famed scenic drives, across the Hachimantai plateau into Akita Prefecture. This thirty-eight-kilometer route is sprinkled with several famous *onsen* that welcome daytrippers dropping in for a quick dip. One worth considering is Goshogake, near the end of the toll road. It's a large establishment that gets more than its share of tour buses but the rustic bathing area boasts a host of tubs, each with a different type of water, and a *rotenburo*. There's also a nice trail behind the inn winding through gurgling volcanic pools and freshwater ponds.

Speaking of trails, from Matsukawa Onsen you can hike in any of several directions into the mountains and to other nearby springs.

Shōfūsō
Matsukawa Onsen, Matsuo-mura, Iwate-ken
PHONE: 01957-8-2245　　　　　　　　　　PRICE: A
TRANSPORTATION: From Morioka Station on the Tohoku Shinkansen, take the bus bound for Matsukawa Onsen for 1 hour and 50 minutes. From Obuke Station on the Hanawa Line, the bus bound for Matsukawa Onsen takes 40 minutes.
　　　BY CAR: From Matsuo-Hachimantai I. C. on the Tohoku Expressway, head west and follow the signs on local roads for 18 kilometers.

✳　✳　✳

Dai Onsen

Dai Onsen is older than its better-known nouveau neighbor just a kilometer down the road, Hanamaki Onsen, whose water it provides. Dai is also one of the few *onsen* towns I like. Compact and quaint, at the end of a little mountain road, it's great for an evening stroll in your *yukata*. Dai's history goes back at least 250 years, when it reputedly was known for a number of common baths.

Resplendent, four-storied Nakajima Ryokan exudes tradition, epitomizing the sensibilities of years gone by. From the outside, it boasts classical lines that few inns can match. Inside, it's extremely laid-back, graceful, and immaculate. The complex, multi-tiered layout and gorgeous, labyrinthine stairways and corridors are captivating. Among the old, unrenovated *onsen* inns we've visited, this is certainly the most elegant.

Ask for the room called "Okina" at the top of the inn. It's actually a superb suite festooned with ornate but tasteful wood-carved shoji and a decent view, especially when there's snow. "Okina" seemed like a lavishly antique penthouse apartment. It has a private toilet, of course, and is absolutely quiet.

The indoor *iwaburo*, or rock bath, is slightly cavern-like with several small pools—attractive, but often very hot. After all, the water comes out of the ground at approximately eighty-nine degrees and isn't mixed with regular water. For milder dips, you can usually sneak pretty easily into the adjoining and more temperate women's bath that features an entirely different but pleasing motif. If you're male and hear women entering the changing room, simply slip back into the *iwaburo*.

Dinner, served in a private tatami-floored room, was sumptuous, replete with top-grade *sashimi*, small but succulent beef steak, hearty *nabe*, and much more. My wife still talks about it. Service here is desirably understated and unintrusive.

From Dai you can traverse the popular eight-kilometer trail over to Namari Onsen (p. 37) from spring to fall. If you have a couple of nights, stay at Nakajima Ryokan, then hike over to Namari the next morning for a memorable dip in the fabled White Monkey bath, and then grab a bus or walk down to Osawa's Kikusuikan (p. 35) for the second night. You'd be hard-pressed to come up with a better three-day hidden hot-spring itinerary.

Nakajima Ryokan
Dai Onsen, 1-190 Dai, Hanamaki-shi, Iwate-ken 025-03
PHONE: 0198-27-2021   PRICE: C, D
TRANSPORTATION: From Shin-Hanamaki Station on the Tohoku Shinkansen, the Dai Onsen-bound bus takes 35 min-
utes.
BY CAR: From Hanamaki I. C. on the Tohoku Jidosha Doro,
follow the signs to Hanamaki Onsen and on to Dai
for a total of about 5 kilometers.

✳   ✳   ✳

Ōsawa Onsen

In an *onsen*-studded district best known for the relatively new
Hanamaki Onsen village, the 200-year-old Osawa preserves the
past better than any rival in the area. Japanese connoisseurs
might tell you that ancient Namari Onsen, just up the road, is of
a higher caliber. The high-ceilinged "White Monkey" bath at
Namari's rambling Fujisan Ryokan is certainly noteworthy (p.
37). But Kikusuikan at Osawa is a much homier choice of lodging, and while Namari lacks a *rotenburo*, Osawa's ranks among
Japan's oldest and most authentic.

Osawa actually comprises three commonly owned inns on the
same undisturbed grounds about a hundred meters below the
main road. The flagship is the modern but stately Sansuikan.
Adjoining it is the rambling *jisuibu*, or self-cooking wing, complete with a compact but amply stocked store. Across the stream
by footbridge, and facing the *rotenburo*, lies the sedate Kikusuikan.
Festooned with a thatched roof and classical landscaping, this
tranquilly elegant remnant of old Japan belongs on a picture
postcard, especially when it's covered with snow.

For a mere 8,000 yen per person (as of 1992), Kikusuikan's
price-to-value ratio is hard to beat. Sure, the unremarkable meals
are served in a utilitarian dining area and the simple rooms
aren't bathroom-equipped. But we found ours, "Umehachi," ac-

commodating in the old style. Ask for this eight-tatami-mat room as it costs no more than the other, six-mat rooms in this wing. If your party is large, ask for one of the spacious and elegant corner rooms on the main building's second floor, which can't possibly disappoint. The staff is wonderfully cordial and unobtrusive. Overall, we felt a tremendous affinity with Kikusuikan and count it among our most pleasing, evocative finds.

Osawa's focal point is the rock-clad, half-roofed *rotenburo* overlooking the river. The water may feel a bit too hot at first but you'll soon get used to it. And there's plenty of crawl-out space for cooling off between dips. Here you'll find lots of bathers from the vicinity—especially after the October harvest when farming families take time to soothe their aches and swap gossip in the local "zuzu" dialect. Mixed bathing is the rule here. Kikusuikan also offers segregated and simple indoor baths with nice views from the opposite side of the river.

If you're traveling by car, multi-*rotenburo* Geto Onsen is within an hour (p. 38). Nearby Namari (p. 37) is only ten minutes away. Dai Onsen (p. 33) is just a half-hour drive.

Kikusuikan
181 Osawa, Yuguchi-aza, Hanamaki-shi, Iwate-ken 025-02
PHONE: 0198-25-2233   PRICE: B
TRANSPORTATION: From Shin-Hanamaki Station on the Tohoku Shinkansen, take the bus for Shin-Namari Onsen for 45 minutes. Get off at Osawa Onsen.
BY CAR: From Hanamaki-Minami I. C. on the Tohoku Jidoshado, follow the signs on local roads for about 10 kilometers.

———————————— ♨ ————————————

Toshichi Onsen

The so-called Aspite Line toll road that winds majestically along the top of Towada-Hachimantai national park between Iwate and Akita prefectures is one of Japan's most magnificent drives, especially in autumn. It's also blessed with *onsen*, including a couple of the most famous in Japan. For my money, the modest Toshichi wins out. Sited a few kilometers below the main road, it is ancient, wooden, idyllically situated, and charmingly rustic. The translucent, sulfurous water doesn't come any better nor more authentically housed. The *rotenburo* at either end of the inn are small but supreme. Heavily traveled as it is, I wouldn't necessarily recommend staying here. But Saiunso is a wonderful drop-in point. If you have time, so is quiet Ofuka Onsen just a bit farther along the Aspite Line from the Iwate side. Log cabin in motif, it's a haven for serious, long-staying bathers in search of therapy. The water is very hot and the pristine surroundings are soothing.

Saiunsō
Kokuyurin, Matsuo-mura, Iwate-gun, Iwate-ken 028-73
Closed in winter.
PHONE: 0195-78-3962   PRICE: A
TRANSPORTATION: From Morioka Station on the Tohoku Shinkansen, take the bus to Horai for 90 minutes. Get off at the Toshichi Onsen stop.

Namari Onsen

A favorite of Japanese *onsen* epicures, this huge and ancient inn is in some ways the centerpiece of the so-called Hanamaki Onsen-go cluster of springs. I prefer Osawa Onsen's Kikusuikan, just down the road (p. 36), because it's more homey and boasts a fine *rotenburo*. But Fujisan's indoor pools are also hard to beat. Especially memorable is the fabled, mixed-bathing White Monkey bath, whose depth of 1.4 meters makes it one of the deepest in Japan. A convenient ledge around the pool's circumference means you don't have to stand up to soak. The cupolaed ceiling must also be one of the country's highest. This is a terrific daytime diversion from Osawa.

Fujisan Ryokan
Namari-aza, Hanamaki-shi, Iwate-ken 025-02
PHONE: 0198-25-2311   PRICE: B
TRANSPORTATION: From Hanamaki Station on the Tohoku Line, the
                bus for Shin Namari Onsen takes 40 minutes. Get
                off at Namari Onsen and walk for 4 minutes.

Getō Onsen

It would be hard to find another *onsen* establishment with a
greater variety of *rotenburo*, each with superb waters from completely different springs. They're spread throughout a large,
undulating precinct. This is bathing near its finest. Unfortunately, the inn is charmless and noisy. Best to drive over for
daytime dipping from Dai or Osawa Onsen (pp. 33, 35), just an
hour away.

Getō Onsen Hotel
Closed from mid-November to mid-May
PHONE: 0197-67-3931   PRICE: B and C
TRANSPORTATION: From Kitakami Station on the Tohoku Shinkansen,
                the bus to Geto takes 1 hour.

Nyūtō Onsen-gō

If one hot spring stands out among Japanese *onsen*, it's Kuroyu. Practically any vernacular book or TV documentary you encounter on hidden hot springs is bound to include images of this archetypal establishment. The rustic complex of thatched-roof buildings nestled into a broad depression at the end of a narrow mountain road could be straight out of a samurai movie. Despite its mere sixty-year history, you'd think Kuroyu dates back centuries. Of the seven springs in Nyuto Onsen-go, this is my top choice.

Walking down the path from a small parking lot you'll soon reach a small dirt clearing with a wood-hewn table and chairs. Off to the side is Kuroyu's inconspicuous office, where you check in. Although the owner is a bit gruff, one of Kuroyu's mellow staffers soon will appear to escort you to your room. It will be simple but cozy, separated from other quarters and the hallway only by sliding *fusuma* doors. That reduces privacy, but tranquillity is the norm and most guests are asleep by 10 P.M. That's good, because you'll be awakened at 7 A.M. for breakfast in the tatami-floored dining area.

Kuroyu's rustic *rotenburo* pavilion is unusually cozy, accommodating just five or six people of both sexes. But we never felt crowded, finding it conducive to quite chats with amiable strangers. Segregated indoor baths are also available in a separate bathhouse. For those wishing to stay for a week or more, Kuroyu boasts an economical *jisuibu* (self-cooking wing).

That might not be a bad idea for budget travelers, since Kuroyu is surrounded by several other hidden springs spread over several dozen square kilometers of verdant mountain territory—the Nyuto Onsen "village." All are within comfortable hiking distance, or a brief bus ride. Most convenient is Magoroku Onsen (p. 43), a five-minute walk down the hill. Magoroku offers a couple of lovely *rotenburo* in a bucolic setting. Drop by the office to pay the modest bathing fee.

Even more alluring than Kuroyu is the much older Tsurunoyu Onsen, so picturesque it easily be a movie set (page 43). But Tsurunoyu unfortunately has placed its *rotenburo* in full view of visitors, who are wont to stare. Nyuto Onsen-go also contains an immaculate *kokumin shukusha* with refreshing showers.

If you've come by car and are staying more than one night, drive back down one evening to Tazawako Kogen Onsen, about halfway to Lake Tazawa. This hot-spring town is unappealing by day but features several charming karaoke bars at night that make for a fun diversion from the time-travel experience of Kuroyu just a few kilometers up the mountain.

Kuroyu Onsen
2-1 Kuroyu, Tazawako-machi, Akita-ken, 014-12
Closed in winter.
PHONE: 0187-46-2214   PRICE: A, B
TRANSPORTATION: At Tazawako Station on the Tazawako Line from Morioka, take the bus for Nyuto Onsen for 55 minutes and get off at the terminus. Walk for 20 minutes.
BY CAR: From Route 341 east of Lake Tazawa, turn at Kashiwayama and drive about 14 kilometers.

✳ ✳ ✳

Doroyu Onsen

Of all the hidden springs I've visited, this is the only one where I was immediately asked my nationality. "Because," the friendly manager said, "we see so few foreigners here that we wonder what sort would find this place." Although it's served by an infrequent bus, this is just about as far off the beaten track as you can get by paved road.

Descending into the remote mountain vale where Doroyu nestles, you know you're onto something special. This quiescent hamlet of no more than a hundred residents can't have changed much in the past fifty years. The only real road is the narrow main street that ends just a few kilometers past town. It's fronted by wooden structures that house three small inns, a tiny food store, and assorted homes. Except for the odd vending machine and the modern roofs, this settlement is right out of Taisho-era Japan. Like Kuroyu (p. 39) it could easily be a movie set.

Of the three lodgings, Okuyama Ryokan is the clear choice. It's a little too hard-edged for my taste, but small and sublimely traditional in most respects. For a place as remote as this, the rooms are bright and airy with little compromise to modernity. The manager proudly told us that ours was the favorite of a famous Japanese actress. I found it amazing that such a luminary had ever found the place.

You'll eat simply but satisfyingly in a tatami-floored dining room, nicely spaced from other guests. The segregated indoor baths are suitably rustic, with cloudy water consistent with the name Doroyu, which means "mud bath." But more appealing is the *kon'yoku* (mixed bathing) *rotenburo* behind the annex across the road. Comprising just a couple of rectangular concrete tubs, it's quiet and unpopulated. The water is crystal-clear and the stars seem within easy reach.

During the daytime, go to the end of the road and hike into another valley for half an hour to an undeveloped spring called Kawarage-yu. Here you'll find several warm, natural pools in an unspoiled setting. The largest one is at the bottom of a striking, hot-spring waterfall. The clothes-changing shelters are ramshackle and open, but who cares? At most, you'll be sharing the entire area with only a couple of other bathers. Buy provisions at the Doroyu store and take them along for a lovely picnic.

The main road to the Doroyu turnoff boasts numerous establishments featuring the famous local specialty—noodles called *inaniwa udon*. They're the best I've eaten in Japan.

Okuyama Ryokan
25 Doroyusawa, Takamatsu, Yuzawa-shi, Akita-ken
Telephone: 0183-79-3021   PRICE: B
TRANSPORTATION: The bus bound for Doroyu Onsen takes 80 minutes from Yuzawa Station on the Ouhansen Line.
          BY CAR: From the prefectural road linking Routes 13 and 398, turn at Kijiyama and drive about 4 kilometers.

Tamagawa Onsen

Although it comprises just one ramshackle inn, this sprawling, isolated complex feels almost like a village and has its own separate grocery store and cafeteria. Given its impersonality and busyness, I wouldn't necessarily recommend staying here. But for a heady daytime bathing experience of the most traditional kind, few places can top Tamagawa. For one thing it boasts what locals call a *jigokudani*, or hell valley—a vast, rocky expanse of sulfuric steam vents and tiny pools of scalding water surrounded by mountains. Here people lie on thin rice-straw mats or blankets to absorb the curative heat and minerals. Then there are the commodious, wooden indoor baths featuring several types and temperatures of water and steam. Mixed bathing is common. This is the major ancient *onsen* mecca of northern Japan.

Tamagawa Onsen
Oaza Tamagawa, Tazawako-machi, Senboku-gun, Akita-ken 014-13
PHONE: 0187-49-2352   PRICE: A
TRANSPORTATION: From Tazawako Station on the Tazawako Line, take the bus bound for Hachimantai Chojo for 90 minutes. Get off at Tamagawa Onsen.

Nyūtō Onsen-gō

Imagine a time-trip back to an Edo-period mountain hamlet and you'll be in Tsurunoyu. Few inns can match this for sheer authenticity. The rustic rooms are unusually arranged one after another at ground level in a long, ancient, wooden building facing onto a broad walkway leading to the spacious *rotenburo*. Each room's entrance is directly off this lane. Unfortunately, the outdoor bath is in an unprotected setting exposed to all visitors. But in the evening, once daytime drop-ins have disappeared, you're in for an ethereal treat.

Tsurunoyu Onsen
Kokuyurin 50, Tazawako-machi, Senboku-gun, Akita-ken, 014-12
Closed in winter.
PHONE: 0187-46-2139   PRICE: B
TRANSPORTATION: From Tazawako Station on the Tazawako Line, take the Nyuto Onsen-bound bus for 50 minutes. Alight at Tsurunoyu Onsen-guchi and walk for 30 minutes.

Nyūtō Onsen-gō

Just a few hundred meters down a trail from Kuroyu lies pastoral, undisturbed Magoroku Onsen. The wooden inn is unremarkable but the mixed-bathing *rotenburo* pools rank among Tohoku's finest. Pristine and boulder-strewn, they lie in a graceful park-like setting that we found irresistible. If you stay at Kuroyu be sure to allow time for a visit here.

Magoroku Onsen
Tazawako-machi, Akita-ken 014-12
PHONE: 0187-46-2224   PRICE: A, B
TRANSPORTATION: See Kuroyu.

Yunokura Onsen

Coursing the waterfall-studded mountain track from Nuruyu Onsen by car and then hiking the steep up-and-down trail to Yunokura for twenty minutes builds one's expectations. You shouldn't be disappointed. At the end of your journey, smack next to a forest stream, lies this special lamp-lit lodging. One of only a half-dozen or so inns left in Japan with no lights, Yueikan is surpassed only by Tashiro Motoyu's Yamadakan in the romantic time-travel department. But it's a lot closer to Tokyo, boasts a better *rotenburo*, and serves decent food.

Yueikan dates back to the late Edo period and has been rebuilt several times since. The current two-story structure was erected in the early Showa years, around 1930. The nicely worn, dark-wood interior bears witness to this sixty-year history. Unfortunately, the ravages of severe winters so damaged the exterior that the management was forced to cover it with aluminum siding. This is less of a detraction than you might imagine.

Your room will be stark, featuring little more than three blemished walls and a fourth made of shoji facing a quiet hallway. The next room may be separated only by sliding *fusuma* doors. But come nightfall, your oil lamp converts your quarters into something amazingly romantic. The overall effect is a hushed atmosphere throughout the inn that mitigates any lack of privacy you may feel. If at all possible, get the upstairs corner room facing the *rotenburo*. It's by far the most serene, private one in the house and offers fine views on two sides.

The Spartan quarters add to the incentive of spending the maximum number of hours in the baths. Indoors, Yueikan offers extremely basic, separate men's and women's baths made of concrete and filled with clear, odorless water. At least they're not tiled! A much better bet is the *kon'yoku rotenburo* (mixed-bathing outdoor bath) about a hundred meters upstream. Large but comfy, it rests next to the stream and below towering trees. All alone in this bath, we watched the moon track across a partly cloudy sky and decided this was as close to nirvana as we might ever come.

The manager told me she limits electrical power in the name of authenticity. The refrigerator runs on propane and the only electricity is from a small generator.

Yueikan
118 Honzawadakeyama, Hanayama-mura, Miyagi-ken 987-25
PHONE: 0228-56-2878   PRICE: B
TRANSPORTATION: From Kurikoma Kogen Station on the Tohoku Shinkansen, the bus to Tsukidate takes 15 minutes. Change to a Hanayama-bound bus for 40 minutes. Get off at Zashu and take a taxi for 40 minutes.
BY CAR: From Tsukidate I. C. on the Tohoku Expressway, take Route 4 north for 3.7 kilometers to Route 398. Turn left and go 31 kilometers to Nuruyu Onsen. Turn right and drive about 4 kilometers. Park at the sign.

✳ ✳ ✳

Gaga Onsen

Huddled in a wide ravine on the massive eastern slope plunging below ski-mecca Zao, this isolated, sprawling, recently renovated inn ranks high in the quality of its modernization. To be sure, it feels more like an enormous, Japanese-style mountain lodge than a typical *ryokan*. Fittingly, the service is cordial but relatively impersonal. Your friendly maid will likely be a young woman who views her role more as a job than a way of life. The pine- and tatami-clad rooms in the new wing, while spacious and pristine, are a tad stark. This is an improvement over the old wing, which tends to be cramped.

But for sheer creature comfort in rugged surroundings, isolated Gaga is hard to beat. Take the salubrious library-cum-salon just across from the simple front desk. Here, free coffee is on offer every morning. Each suite-like room in the new wing sports a refrigerator and Western-style bathroom but is otherwise unremittingly Japanese. The unobtrusive service, along with meals in a dining room, make for plenty of privacy in your own quarters. Yet in obeisance to its antecedents, the management has retained a self-cooking *jisuibu*.

Gaga's special magic is its baths, and you've got four wonderful ones to choose from. The capacious main *ofuro*, separated by sex, resonate with the scent of the cedar that bedecks them. Each offers two large tubs of differing temperatures in separate, high-ceilinged rooms. Scattered around the edges are wooden pillows that invite you to recline in between immersions. Broad windows look out over the river that defines the valley, offering splended views.

If you think that aromatic cedar is just about the finest fragrance you've ever whiffed, disabuse yourself by trundling over to the old wing's smallish *hinoki* baths. *Hinoki* is cypress, and to the Japanese no wood scent is more sublime. You'll probably agree. Expensive and maintenance-intensive, *hinoki* has become a rare luxury.

Then there's the mixed-bathing *rotenburo*. Though not one of Japan's finest, it's certainly above average. At night the view across the river toward the nicely illuminated, craggy far bank is memorable. The meaning of Gaga—rugged—will immediately come to mind. Finally, check out the *kazokuburo*, or family bath. This larger-than-normal, extremely comfortable and intimate suite is perfect for privacy-seeking couples.

The food at Gaga most likely won't win any awards, though it's perfectly adequate. Take advantage of eating in the dining room which will allow you to meet the other guests and get out of your room.

Remote though it is, Gaga enjoys wide repute among Japanese. Although that does mean lots of daytime drop-ins, thanks to enlightened management, these daytrippers are confined to the *hinoki* baths, preserving the ambience of the main and outdoor pools for staying guests.

Gaga Onsen
1 Gaga, Aza Maekawa, Kawasaki-cho, Shibata-gun, Miyagi-ken
PHONE: 0224-87-2021   PRICE: B, C
TRANSPORTATION: Take the Tohoku Shinkansen to Shiroishi Zao. The bus for Togatta Onsen takes 50 minutes. From there, a taxi or prearranged, inn-provided microbus takes 20 minutes.
BY CAR: From Shiroishi or Murata I. C. on the Tohoku Jidosha Doro, follow the signs to Togatta Onsen for about 18 kilometers. Drive another 5.5 kilometers to Aone Onsen and pick up the signs for Gaga, about 5 kilometers away.

Fukiage Onsen

Arriving here in a blizzard at 7:30 p.m., thanks to a collision that made us several hours late, we couldn't have received a warmer, more understanding welcome. Our room was simple, as was the food, but the solicitude of the manager and his staff makes this an inviting place. Hounkaku lies isolated at the bottom of a steep hill in the small Fukiage enclave. Counterbalancing its rather prosaic architecture are nicely designed indoor baths with panoramic windows and a commodious *rotenburo* next to a small waterfall. If the water is too hot in the latter, as it was for us, the management will helpfully open a cold-water pipe. Nearby Todoroki Onsen has a luxuriously landscaped, secluded *rotenburo* that's well worth visiting.

Hōunkaku
Aza Fukiage, Onikobe, Narugo-machi, Miyagi-ken 989-69
PHONE: 0229-86-2243   PRICE: B
TRANSPORTATION: From Narugo Station on the Riku-u Higashi Line,
take the bus to Onikobe for 30 minutes. Then walk
for 15 minutes.

Yunodai Onsen

Way up what turned out the next day to be an unusually pan-oramic road, compact Yumotoya proved a snug and welcoming haven when we arrived after dark in a driving rainstorm. Little frogs hopping around the entrance and the aroma of burning firewood testified to the far-mountain surroundings.

We wound up being the only guests on a mid-October week-night. The friendly proprietress, who runs homey little Yumotoya by herself, made us feel like family. Soon after tucking us into our room, putting out dinner in another, and explaining that her octogenarian mother was somewhere on the premises, she apolo-getically took her leave to attend to some kind of business away from the inn. It must have been important, given the inclement weather.

Her absence gave us the chance to explore the deserted place. It looked largely unused. The next morning, the owner confirmed that her guests are few and almost entirely *joren*, or perennials. She doesn't seek or even encourage newcomers. Indeed, when I phoned for reservations she tried to talk me out of coming, claiming that her humble inn was too primitive for any foreigner to appreciate.

That turned out not to be prejudice but honest modesty and a lack of staff. During subsequent phone calls and after our arrival, the owner was exceptionally friendly and accommodating. What is more, Yumotoya proved remarkably clean, appealing, and comfortable.

Rarely have I eaten so well at an inn for so little money. Dinner was an enormous sliced-beef and vegetable *jingisukan ryori* that we grilled ourselves, the best broiled herring and *mazegohan* I've ever tasted, exotic stuffed *akebi* (a wild, fruit-like vegetable), braised wild mushrooms, and a huge pot of *oden*. For breakfast we feasted on hot, large cups of *chawanmushi*, warm corn and potato fritters, and fresh fruit along with the usual *misoshiru* and rice. Both meals were served in a guest room next to our own.

The tiny wooden bath of muddy, artificially heated water can handle only one soaker at a time. That was no problem for a twosome: while one of us showered the other steeped. The heavy-duty mineral water felt terrific.

Ask for the simple but homey room at the end of the hall near the kitchen and across from the toilet. It's a bit noisy in the morning while breakfast is being readied but faces onto a small, modest garden above an invisible but soothingly audible stream.

Yumotoya
8-1 Yunodai, Yawata-machi, Hokai-gun, Yamagata-ken
PHONE: 0234-64-4703 PRICE: A
TRANSPORTATION: From Sakata Station on the Uetsu Line, take the bus to Kannonji for 25 minutes. Transfer to the bus for Ryoko Mura and ride for 30 minutes. (This bus runs only in July and August. At other times, take a taxi.)
BY CAR: From Kannonji just east of Route 345 on Route 344, turn north and follow the signs for about 20 kilometers.

Ginzan **Onsen**

This picturesque hamlet at the end of a deep-mountain road once drew mainly a serious-bathing crowd. But some years back it became the setting for a wildly popular TV soap opera called "Oshin," and tourists have flocked to it ever since. Ginzan has retained most of its character and serenity, though, and is well worth a visit. The settlement's narrow thoroughfare, lined with gorgeous old inns and bisected by a stream, is too tiny for cars to negotiate. Unfortunately, the inns don't quite live up to their potential. Best known is the four-hundred-year-old Notoya, whose ornate four-story façade and cupola are among the most famous of *onsen* images. Run by the seventeenth generation of the founding Kido family, it's a welcoming place. But there's little inside to suggest its antiquity. Floors and stairways are linoleum, the rooms are nondescript, and we ate in a private room with a kitschy coffee-shop decor. At least dinner was tasty—warm, grilled rockfish on skewers, delicious raw *yamame*, a luscious chicken *nabe*, braised carp, tempura, and more. The baths, once tile, now are of immaculate *hinoki* and incredibly steamy. The mineral-redolent water isn't outrageously hot. Below the lobby there's a murky, cave-like bath that can hold about four. Although the baths and food weren't as good, we liked our room better at cheaper Gensenkan across the way. At either place, be sure to specify rooms in front. Be warned that inns here don't allow daytime dipping, but there's a modest *kyodoburo* (public bath) for drop-ins.

Notoya Ryokan
Ginzan, Ohanazawa-shi, Yamagata-ken 999-43
PHONE: 0237-28-2327   PRICE: C, D
TRANSPORTATION: From Oishida Station on the Ou Line, the bus to Ohanazawa Machiaishitsu takes 10 minutes. From there, it's a 35-minute bus ride to Ginzan Onsen.

Asahi Kōsen
Of the two remote *kosen* in this wilderness quarter of Yamagata-ken, Asahi is the clear choice. Kodera Kosen, the other alternative, is more typically Japanese, but offers few charms to offset its Spartan quarters. Cozy and rustic Asahi carries the overtones of a mellowly managed, Western-style mountain lodge, with its ancient log beams and wood-burning stove complementing a spacious, atmospheric lounge complete with a loft. Other ameni-

ties include a Western-style toilet, freshly brewed coffee, and quiet jazz. All of which come as a surprise at the end of a tortuous, twenty-kilometer unpaved road. The guest rooms are basic and the bath of mud-colored water is modest, but as much as I grumbled about the difficult drive, I'd go back in a flash. When reserving, be sure to specify the main building.

Asahi Onsen Naturalist no Ie
Tatsuki, Asahi-machi, Nishimurayama-gun, Yamagata-ken
PHONE: 0237-67-3589   PRICE: A
TRANSPORTATION: From Yamagata Station, take the bus to Miyajuku for 85 minutes. Change at the terminus to the bus for Asahi Kosen, a 70-minute ride. (The latter bus runs only in summer and Asahi is closed in winter).

Namekawa Onsen

This ramshackle complex is a bit prosaic from the outside, but its rugged surroundings, quietude, alluring baths, and rustic interiors more than compensate. Resting beside a boulder-strewn rivulet all on its own, Fukushimaya is one of your better mountain getaways. The nearest other structure (Ubayu) is a good three kilometers away. We found the indoor men's bath fully integrated sexually. But only the males seemed prepared to brave the rocky *rotenburo* in the blustery, rainy weather prevalent during our visit. All in all a richly traditional and relaxed place.

Fukushimaya
Aza Namekawa, Oaza Osawa, Yonezawa-shi, Yamagata-ken 992-13
PHONE: 0238-34-2250   PRICE: A
TRANSPORTATION: From Fukushima on the Tohoku Shinkansen, take the Ou Line to Toge. A prearranged inn bus will get you there in 15 minutes.

Ubayu Onsen

If not for some difficulties we encountered with the staff, this spectacular spring would rate a full entry. Compact and pristine Masugataya huddles against a remote cliffside at the end of a long, precarious road that climbs relentlessly into a mountain aerie on the Yamagata-Fukushima border. Just a short stroll above the Spartan, lodge-like inn, lie two lovely *rotenburo*, the *kon'yoku* of which offers breathtaking views of the dramatically rugged surroundings. Vistas don't come much better. You can often see Japanese *kamoshika* antelope coursing the cliffs across the rushing river. The sulfuresque, cobalt-blue water is just the right temperature for long soaks in chilly autumn weather. To avoid the staff that almost literally kicked us out of bed at 7:15 A.M. for breakfast (among other sins), a better bet is to stay at the friendlier Namekawa Onsen three kilometers down the mountain (see above) and visit Ubayu for a daytime dip.

Masugataya
Closed in winter.
PHONE: 0238-35-2633   PRICE: B
TRANSPORTATION: Take the Tohoku Shinkansen to Fukushima, then catch the infrequent Ou Line run to Toge. Masugataya will pick you up there on prearrangement. From Namekawa Onsen, hitchhike or walk about an hour.

Shirabu Onsen

Shirabu is an evocative compound of three chockablock inns that feel like one ancient complex but are separately managed. Best known is Higashiya, or the East Inn. It's wonderfully traditional, replete with a thatched roof and comfy indoor baths. Next-door is Nakaya, or the Middle Inn, which features fine and lively wooden baths just off a lovely courtyard. Facing the road is the nicest of the lot—Nishiya, or the West Inn. It's more modern and exposed to traffic than its neighbors but quite beautiful.

Nishiya Ryokan
Oaza Seki 1537, Yonezawa-shi, Yamagata-ken 992-14
PHONE: 0238-55-2211. Higashiya, 0238-55-2011. Nakaya, 0238-55-2121   PRICE: D
TRANSPORTATION: From Yonezawa Station on the Ou Line, the bus for Shirabu Onsen takes 50 minutes.

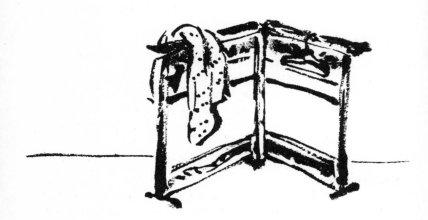

Oku Tsuchiyu Onsen

Tsuchiyu Onsen is one of Fukushima Prefecture's larger *onsen* towns, a playground for the nearby city of Fukushima with a predictable lack of grace. Yet just a kilometer beyond lies the relatively isolated Kawakami, one of three inns strung along a narrow mountain road above Tsuchiyu. From the outside it's nothing special, but once you've settled in, its charms gradually become apparent.

Start with the attentive staff. Our maid was an elderly woman whose Tohoku accent was so thick that I had to have her repeat almost everything she said. She, likewise, interpreted my explanation that I was a journalist to mean that I worked for JR (Japan Railways). Perhaps because I'm a foreigner—not to mention the 2,000 yen we tipped her at the outset—she served us our meals in our room while other guests were relegated to the dining room. The food, by the way, was superior and we weren't surprised when people in town told us the proprietor, Abe-san, is known for his assiduous gathering of wild-vegetable delicacies.

Then come the baths. Kawakami Onsen is blessed with such an abundance of naturally hot water that it boasts one of the largest indoor baths in the region. This appropriately is called Senninburo, or the "Thousand-Person Bath." Aesthetic it's not, but the water is agreeable and you certainly won't bump up against fellow bathers. Much more charming is the large, roof-clad *rotenburo*, which extends into a spacious cave that affords plenty of privacy. The water here is so hot that management keeps two cold-water hoses running to prevent scalding. On a cold winter day we found the temperature just right, but I suspect that in summer it could be unpleasantly hot. The inn also features two cozy *kazokuburo*, or family baths, that can accommodate two people at a time. One is hotter than the other so test them both before choosing.

We were surprised in this part of Japan to find that both of the main baths have separate times for men's and women's bathing. But we also discovered that enlightened couples get around this by simply going in at the hours designated for men. One afternoon in the *rotenburo* we encountered a thirty-something, uninhibited Japanese couple who offered us saké and pleasant conversation.

When reserving, specify the *kyukan*, or old wing, which offers traditional rooms. The second floor seemed to be the best.

Near as it is to Fukushima City, Kawakami only gets about ten foreign guests a year, Mrs. Abe told us, most brought by Japanese friends. Even more off the beaten track is the archetypal and isolated Fudoyu Onsen (below), a fifteen-minute drive up a tortuous mountain track above Tsuchiyu and Kawakami and well worth a pop-in. If not for its tiny, tepid baths it would be a main entry in this guide.

Kawakami Onsen

Kawakami 3, Tsuchiyu Onsen Machi, Fukushima-shi, Fukushima-ken

PHONE: 0245-95-2136   PRICE: B

TRANSPORTATION: The bus from Fukushima Station to Tsuchiyu Onsen takes 40 minutes. From there, walk for 20 minutes or hop a cab.

BY CAR: From Fukushima-nishi I. C. on the Tohoku Jidoshado, take Route 115 west for 11.5 kilometers to Tsuchiyu. Turn into town, pass through it and drive 1 kilometer.

———————————— ♨ ————————————

Fudōyu Onsen

A quintessentially rustic, hidden spring, this treasure is definitely worth negotiating the slightly harrowing mountain track that leads up for several kilometers from concretized Tsuchiyu Onsen. Enveloped by dense vegetation on the slope of a steep ravine, Fudoyu is the picture of a forgotten Japan. Unfortunately, its small baths, including a tiny but memorable *rotenburo*, suffer from a paucity of hot water. Your best bet is to stay at Kawakami Onsen (p. 56) down below and hike or drive up for a daytime dip.

Fudōyu Onsen
Ozasa 25, Tsuchiyu Onsen Machi, Fukushima-shi, Fukushima-ken
PHONE: 0245-95-2002   PRICE: A
TRANSPORTATION: Take the bus from Fukushima Station for Tsuchiyu
                Onsen for 40 minutes. Hike 30 minutes up a trail or
                take a taxi for 15 minutes.

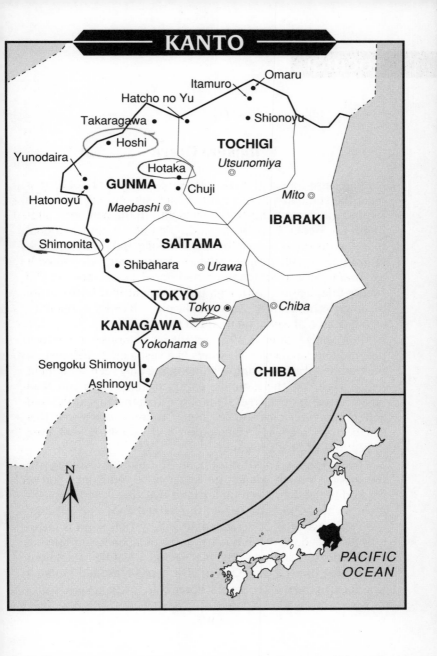

Itamuro **Onsen**

Finding *onsen* inns within easy striking distance of Tokyo that meet the standards of this guide is difficult. Among those I've located, this unique hostelry comes fifth in the pantheon after Kajika-an, Hoshi, Kaya no Ie, and Shimonita. Less traditional than the others, it is nonetheless a striking and pleasing modernization. My American companion appropriately described it as "avant-garde traditional, or traditional Japan meeting the twenty-first century." Although purists might find Daikokuya a bit contrived and flawed, we loved the place. It certainly qualifies as the pearl of development-crazed Nasu.

Thoroughly redone in 1991, Daikokuya comprises three low-rise, modern Japanese-style wings in a vast garden area just off the traditional *onsen* village of Itamuro, the only such settlement left in Nasu. At the grounds' entrance, those who can read Japanese will spot discreet signs suggesting that big parties and golfers aren't welcome and describing the inn as *hoyo to tenji*. This can be translated as "recuperation and exhibition"—alluring indications of what's to come.

And Daikokuya doesn't disappoint. The gardens leading up to the *genkan*, though young, are imaginative. And once you've entered the *genkan*, you'll understand that this is an establishment for those who appreciate the refined and sophisticated. Resembling a large, understated art gallery, Daikokuya is tastefully festooned with high-quality pieces of Japanese art ranging from prints to sculptures. The management features a different artist three times a year. On our visit it was Masanari Murai, a woodblock-print master. Several dozen of his distinguished works graced walls throughout the inn and were available for purchase.

Rooms are priced according to their wing: 17,000 yen per person in Umenokan, 16,000 yen in Takenokan, and 14,000 yen in Matsunokan. We chose Umenokan and were enchanted. In the farthest reaches of the complex, the restful two-story structure faces a secluded garden just beyond the *rotenburo*. Richly carpeted halls with traditional wooden ceilings lend an air of luxury. Our lovely room for two was fully ten mats, plus toilet and an engaging kitchenette-table-and-chair arrangement where meals were served. The food, unfortunately, barely rose above typical *ryokan* fare.

The baths are plentiful and delightful. In addition to the bright, airy main baths are a compact but nicely rendered *kon'yoku rotenburo* and aromatic *hinoki* baths. The latter are particularly evocative at night, facing a small, dimly lit garden. But here's where you'll find some flaws. In the *hinoki* bath, unlike those in some other inns, only the tub itself is made from this expensive wood. The main baths are paneled in fake wood.

All in all, though, this is a wonderfully approachable place for Westerners seeking a tasteful Japanese experience with a full range of amenities, privacy, space, and an extra-special touch. Adjacent Itamuro village itself isn't much, but Daikokuya is sufficiently removed.

Daikokuya
856 Itamuro, Kuroiso-shi, Tochigi-ken 325-01
PHONE: 0287-69-0226   PRICE: C, D
TRANSPORTATION: From Kuroiso Station on the Tohoku Line, the bus for Itamuro Onsen takes 35 minutes.
BY CAR: From Nishinasuno Shiobara I. C. on the Tohoku Jidoshado, take Route 400 northwest for 6 kilometers to local road No. 29. Turn right for 9.5 kilometers then turn left at Toda and drive about 8 kilometers.

✳ ✳ ✳

Shionoyu Onsen

One of Japan's better-known and less-attractive hot-spring towns is Tochigi-ken's Shiobara, whose environs comprise no less than a dozen separate *onsen* and several dozen hostelries of questionable appeal. Yet sitting just a kilometer above the hoi polloi is the sedate, three-inn enclave of Shionoyu. It could just as easily be ten or one hundred kilometers away. For a quick weekend out of Tokyo it's well worth checking out.

There's one main reason: the *rotenburo*. No two outdoor baths are the same, of course, but Myogaya's is uniquely fetching. To get there means negotiating several very steep, covered staircases plunging from the inn to the depths of the Kanomata River gorge. Near the bottom you'll first encounter the separate men's and women's changing rooms. Off to the left, and on about the same level, are several *goemonburo*, cramped, vat-like tubs that barely accommodate a single bather. They're named for a legendary figure who was boiled alive in a similar pot.

Descend one more short stairway and you're at the sexually integrated bath-site. Here you'll find four sheltered tubs: two smallish but comfortable wooden ones implanted in cement, a larger one of concrete to the back, and a tiny cave-like pool off to the side. All face onto the narrow river, a gurgling mountain stream that's just a hop away. Its other side soars almost vertically, clad in thick vegetation. This ranks among the best outdoor bathing we've enjoyed anywhere.

Somehow, Myogaya's *rotenburo* manages to combine a sense of both coziness and spaciousness, solitude and fraternity. Rarely crowded in our experience, the baths can be more or less your own private playground if you time things right. That means when everyone else is having dinner or after 10:00 A.M.

The inn itself is nothing to brag about. The wooden main building, which clings to the top of the gorge, is charmingly decrepit. None of the simple rooms has its own toilet. Some in the concrete annex do, but those quarters are even more banal.

Meals are boilerplate and entirely forgettable. But if you can obtain a gorge-facing room in the main building, the view and the *rotenburo* below will make up for the various deficiencies. This shouldn't be too hard: we've found Myogaya relatively easy to reserve for Saturdays on short notice.

Though I generally eschew *onsen* inns with *karaoke* bars, Myogaya's is just funky enough to be tolerable—nay, enjoyable. Maybe that's because the assembled strangers asked me for an encore.

Myōgaya Honkan

353 Shimo-Shiobara, Shiobara-machi, Nasu-gun, Tochigi-ken 329-29

PHONE: 02873-2-2831 PRICE: B

TRANSPORTATION: Take the Tohoku Shinkansen to Nasu-Shiobara. Change to the Shiobara Onsen bus and ride for 45 minutes to the Shiokama stop. Then walk for 15 minutes, or catch a taxi.

BY CAR: From Nishinasuno-Shiobara I. C. on the Tohoku Expressway, take Route 400 for about 14 kilometers to Fukuwata Onsen. Turn left at the sign and drive for 1 kilometer.

Ōmaru Onsen

Nestled in a quiet depression just off a main road, Omaru is surprisingly secluded for Nasu and is one of the best bets in this massive and highly developed resort area. Tastefully modern in the Japanese style, Omaru's rooms are supremely comfortable. The food is bountiful and first-rate. Few inns boast as many private *kazokuburo*, or family baths, and the separate men's and women's *rotenburo* are spacious. If there's time, wander down to the rustic and secluded Kita Onsen and try its famous but modest waterfall bath. Rustic Kita would rate an entry here but for a major sin: the incongruous preponderance of bathing suits in its exposed, swimming pool-sized *rotenburo*. Nearby Benten Onsen has a pavilioned *rotenburo* worth checking out.

Ōmaru Onsen Ryokan
269 Yumoto, Nasu-machi, Nasu-gun, Tochigi-ken 325-03
PHONE: 0287-76-3050   PRICE: C, D
TRANSPORTATION: From Kuroiso Station on the Tohoku Line, take the bus bound for Ropeway by way of Nasu Yumoto for 55 minutes. Alight at Omaru Onsen and walk about 5 minutes.

Okukinu Onsen-gō
Okukinu Onsen-go is probably the most popular (and maybe the best-preserved) wilderness hot-spring enclave in Japan. The only way in is by a long hike over a dirt road or via infrequent four-wheel-drive escort vans provided by a couple of the inns. Among the four widely scattered springs, each with a single ryokan, rustic Hatcho no Yu offers probably the finest combination of setting and *rotenburo*. The convivial outdoor baths are technically segregated but *kon'yoku* isn't uncommon. This is superb outdoor bathing. Unfortunately, the ramshackle inn is mundane, and noisy on weekends. The three relatively nearby springs are also worth a short hike. Nearest is Kaniyu—egregiously renovated some years ago—whose hot *rotenburo* are pleasant. Much closer to my heart are the wonderfully rustic Nikkozawa and Teshirozawa. They didn't gain an entry here mainly because they don't provide transport, which means a long hike.

Hatchō no Yu
874 Kawamata, Kuriyama-mura, Tochigi-ken 321-27
PHONE: 0288-96-0306   PRICE: B
TRANSPORTATION: From Kinugawa Onsen Station on the Tobu Line, the Meotobuchi Onsen-bound bus takes 2 hours. Walk for about 90 minutes or phone in advance to learn when Hatcho's van leaves Meotobuchi.

Hōshi Onsen

Not only is this one of Japan's top hidden *onsen* inns, it's within easy striking distance of Tokyo. Only Nanadaru's Kajika-an and Hotaka's Kaya no Ie can make the same claim. While I rank them slightly higher, the much older Chojukan may come closer to the Platonic form of the ideal hidden spring. This is epitomized by the classic wooden bathhouse. Sporting a multi-tiered, wood-shingled roof with soaring cupola and dramatically raftered interior, it's no wonder photos of this edifice have become the icon of the quintessential *onsen* bath.

The spacious bathhouse belies the notion that *onsen* have to be intolerably hot. Chojukan's is so comfortable that it's easy to lose track of time as you luxuriate in the water. Of the four adjoining cypress tubs, the two near the windows are less hot than the two closer to the entrance. But be careful. On our first visit I missed the warning sign about over-soaking. The next day I was completely sapped, a victim of deceptively strong minerals. The Japanese call it *yu-zukare*. Next-door is a smaller bath for women. But unlike virtually every other *onsen* in this part of Japan, mixed bathing is common in the main bath. This is made easier by ethereal, dim lighting at night that keeps most bathers hidden in shadows.

Exquisitely complementing the bathhouse is the adjacent log-beamed main building dating 300 years back to the Edo period. An annex at the back blends in perfectly and a newer wing across from the *genkan* exterior meticulously preserves ancient sensibilities.

Sitting pristinely alone at the end of a long, narrow road in the middle of a primeval forest, Chojukan has fended off much of the

.wentieth century. (A small ski slope about a kilometer away and a TV and vending machines in the lobby are the biggest threats.) We have the enlightened management of the youngish Mr. and Mrs. Okamura to thank for this preservation. Mr. Okamura is the sixth-generation owner and is an avowed conservationist. Most mornings, his charming wife, Aiko, serves tea and sometimes coffee around the unstintingly traditional hearth just off the entryway.

Rooms in the older quarters tend to lack private toilets and can be a bit noisy in the morning as maids scurry along the ancient corridors arranging breakfast. If your party is four or more, ask for the largest room on the second floor of the original building—it's redolent of antiquity. Although the new wing is luxurious and serene, with in-room facilities including kitchenettes, it exceeds my price ceiling.

In any event, Hoshi's fine food won't leave you longing to cook for yourself. While not particularly lavish, the satisfying meals are prepared with superior ingredients and a touch of élan. The simple but sublime turtle *nabe* stew, for example, was rare and most pleasing.

Chōjukan

650 Nagai, Niiharu-mura, Tone-gun, Gunma-ken 379-14
PHONE: 0278-66-0005   PRICE: C, D
TRANSPORTATION: From Jomo Kogen Station on the Joetsu Shinkan-sen, it's a 30-minute bus ride to Sarugakyo Onsen. Change to a bus or taxi for Hoshi Onsen, about 20 minutes away.
BY CAR: From Tsukiyono I. C. on the Kanetsu Jidoshado, take Route 17 northwest for about 17.5 kilometers. Turn left at the sign for Hoshi and drive for another 5 kilometers.

✳ ✳ ✳

Hotaka Onsen

For pure authenticity in a recent renovation, Kaya no Ie surpasses even Kajika-an. The long, steep, multi-tiered roof is thatched. The broad, deep *genkan* is hard-packed dirt, with soaring rafters and heated by a traditional wood-burning stove. A kettle dangles over a smoldering *irori* in the tatami lounge. There's not a vending machine in the place, nor a TV or piece of carpet. The capacious bath is *hinoki* throughout. The young manager and his wife dress in traditional peasant garb.

Built in the early 1980s by a nearby junior college of arts, nonprofit Kaya no Ie is a wonderfully successful attempt to preserve ancient sensibilities. Containing just seven guest rooms in an imposing structure, it's serene, personal, and uncrowded.

If at all possible, reserve the one *tokubetsu shitsu*, or special room. For just 20% more per person it's significantly better than the other rooms, which are perfectly fine in their own right. Also known as "Toga no O," the special room is actually a suite comprising a six-mat living room with a large *kotatsu*, a copper tea-ceremony basin, and exquisite shoji overlooking the *genkan*. The walls are dark tan and accented with light and dark wood. The sloping ceiling makes this room especially cozy. The ten-mat bedroom boasts the first shoji skylight I've ever seen but otherwise is elegantly spare. The floors throughout the suite are heated and known as *yuka danbo* in Japanese.

Then there's the private *hinoki* bath that can easily accommodate two and has a shoji skylight. Just outside the bath, the refrigerator contained a healthy supply of ice and Ebisu beer. The toilet was warm and Western. The only flaw noticeable in the entire suite is the incongruous plastic sink unit. If you can't go when this room is available, the regular rooms contain eight mats, a sitting area, Western toilet, and a sink. They're tasteful, high-ceilinged, and have striking wood-and-shoji chandeliers.

For dinner, make your way to the charming *shokudo* (dining hall) through the wide, dark-planked corridors. In winter they're suffused with the delicate aroma of burning wood. At the *shokudo*, you'll sit on tatami or on tatami benches at a single enormous wood-slab table. The food here is rigorously vegetarian. That's right, not even fish. We enjoyed the soy milk, warm mountain-vegetable tempura, barley soup, brown rice, and other taste sensations. This is a nicely prepared but simple meal.

Kaya no Ie's main bath must have been inspired by Hoshi's. The large, square, sunken tub sits in the middle of a *hinoki*-planked floor and under massive beams supporting a vaulted roof. The walls are almost entirely windows. The water is clear, odorless, and fine. Turn down the lights at night and this is premier bathing.

The inn's only downside is its proximity to the road. But what little traffic there is moves quietly and there are no other buildings around.

Kaya no Ie
2077-1 Kawaba Yuhara, Kawaba-mura, Tone-gun, Gunma-ken 378-01
PHONE: 0278-52-2220   PRICE: C, D
TRANSPORTATION: With prior arrangement, Kaya no Ie will pick you up from Jomo Kogen Station on the Joetsu Shinkansen.
BY CAR: From Numata I. C. on the Kanetsu Jidoshado, follow the signs to Kawaba Onsen for about 9 kilometers. Continue on the same road for 4 kilometers to Hotaka.

✳ ✳ ✳

Chūji Onsen

Kunisada Chuji was one of the most celebrated gangsters of the Edo Period, a precursor of today's *yakuza*. It was in this arduous mountain quarter of Gunma that he hid out, and it is for him that this spring was named.

Until 1993, Chujikan was a nondescript two-story inn with few bragging rights. Then, an enlightened management tore the place down and replaced it with one of the most alluring remakes I've come across. The new Chujikan pulls off a splendid farmhouse motif, meticulous down to the exposed wiring and ceramic insulators running along the ceilings. Stone basins with bamboo spigots for hand-washing grace the *shokudo* entrance and stone-floored toilets. Nothing about the place seems forced or contrived.

The only structure at Chuji, the single-story, half-timbered Chujikan sprawls along a quiet wilderness road. Step through the portals and you're in Edo-era Japan. The large, high-raftered *genkan* is strewn with wooden farming implements, straw capes and snowshoes, and several huge vases of fresh flowers. To the left is the *irori* room with views over the inn's garden-to-be. To the right sits the ponderous front desk with nary an electronic implement in sight.

The perky *okami-san* led us down perhaps the longest, most emotive corridor I've traversed at an inn. Planked with dark wood and high-raftered like the *genkan*, it turned out to be ethereally lit at night. Our comely room, "Hidekichi no Ma," was named—like Chujikan's others—for one of Kunisada Chuji's lieutenants. As it rests at the end of the hall, near the baths and facing the garden, I'd recommend it.

Comprising ten tatami mats, a small sitting area with *zabuton* cushions, and a dark-wood sink and Japanese-toilet area, it was dark beige and half-timbered. The very tall ceiling was also dark-raftered and beamed. All the lights were incandescent, as were almost all at Chujikan. The only incongruous nod to the late twentieth century was a VCR and a small library of videotapes.

Chujikan's aesthetically tiled indoor baths are perfectly acceptable and face onto a nicely illuminated garden. But you're much better off in the mixed-bathing *rotenburo*. There are actually separate tubs for men and women but they're smack-dab against each other and unfenced. The far edge of these pretty pools looks over a charming waterfall in a deep ravine that's nicely spotlighted at night. And the *rotenburo* itself is partially illuminated by large gas-torches. The clear, odorless water is artificially heated to a very warm but not uncomfortable point. The boiler shuts off before bedtime.

Dinner here is a delight, announced by the beating of a drum. Served in a rustic, vaulted-ceiling dining room, each course of the meal was explained by the burly woman cook. We feasted on carp and *konnyaku sashimi* with an unusually tasty sauce, a monster *inoshishi*, and chicken *nabe* stew that contained real wild boar rather than the half-pork, half-boar meat used by most inns; broiled trout; a lip-smacking gruel of tofu, mushrooms and ground meat; cold spinach with peanut sauce; tempura; *mazegohan*; and more.

This is probably the best *onsen* bargain within easy reach of Tokyo. One tip: parties of two or three are normally assigned one of the eight-mat rooms facing the road so try to go as a foursome if possible.

> **Chūjikan**
> Miyagi-mura, Seta-gun, Gunma-ken 371-02
> PHONE: 0272-83-3015   PRICE: B, D (the latter for a
> nice *hanare*, or cottage, but not worth so much more).
> TRANSPORTATION: From Asakusa, take the Tobu Line to Akagi Station, then a taxi for 30 minutes.
> BY CAR: From Akagi I. C. on the Kanetsu Jidosha Doro, take local road No. 51 toward Akagi-san for about 20 kilometers to the Miyosawa intersection. Turn left and drive for about 3 kilometers.

✳ ✳ ✳

Shimonita Onsen

The flinty town of Shimonita and its surrounding area in Gunma Prefecture's obscure southwest corner is known for its green onions and *konnyaku*, the rubbery, glutinous globs used heavily in *oden* and sukiyaki. Shimonita is also at the foot of an alluring saw-toothed mountain that can be seen for miles around.

Sedate Seiryuso's complex of main building, cottages, *rotenburo*, ponds, fish pools, covered walkways, and streams make it hard to believe that you're only five minutes from a sizable town. Yet tucked up into a quiet mountain hollow less than two kilometers from bustling Shimonita, isolated Seiryuso is tranquillity in spades. It's also a bargain. For here you can reserve your own *hanare*, or traditional cottage, at a very reasonable price.

The best is probably "Ike Sanso," which overlooks a lovely pond. Ours, called "Sansuiso," was more cloistered and next to a gurgling brook. A bit scruffy, it contained a six-tatami-mat main room, three-tatami-mat utility area, Japanese toilet, and sink. Nothing special decor-wise, but the solitude made up for any deficiencies.

The baths here rank near the top. Although the clear, odorless water comes out of the ground at a chilly twelve degrees, it's plenty warm by the time it reaches the tubs. A bit too warm, perhaps, especially in the *rotenburo*. But the segregated outdoor pools are beautifully laid out, bedecked with boulders and perched over a densely vegetated stream. A pretty pavilion nicely integrates the changing areas and pools.

Getting to the indoor baths from the *hanare* or *rotenburo* is a bit of a walk but well worth the effort. Their water is less hot and they're done up in delightful *hinoki* (cypress). One nice touch is the terra-cotta tiled roof atop the wooden wall separating the men's and women's baths. Large bay windows look out toward the stream and road.

On the way to and from them you pass through an interesting area of sunken tanks and pools, each housing a different species of fish.

You also traverse the main garden, which I never got tired of visiting. It boasts an unusually large pond and a couple of charming bridges.

Dinner was a simple affair of raw carp, *konnyaku sashimi*, a light *inoshishi nabe*, broiled *yamame*, and the usual trimmings. It was served in our *hanare* by a delightful grandmotherly type, as was breakfast.

The welcome and service at Seiryuso are warm and natural. For an inn so close to Tokyo, it's a remarkably down-home experience to stay here.

Seiryūsō
769 Yoshizaki, Shimonita-machi, Gunma-ken
PHONE: 0274-82-3077   PRICE: C
TRANSPORTATION: From Shimonita Station on the Joshin Dentetsu Line, a taxi takes 5 minutes.
BY CAR: From Shimonita I. C. on the Joshinetsu Expressway, take Route 254 for about 4 kilometers to Shimonita and look for the sign on the left.

Takaragawa Onsen

Once one of my favorites, this increasingly popular inn has caved in to big-time commercialism. Its enormous *rotenburo* remain among Japan's finest and the setting is secluded. But on weekends it's chockablock, including motorcycle-gang drop-ins and more Westerners than you're likely to spot in central Tokyo. Prices, given the humdrum food and general lack of private toilets, are exorbitant and a new wing has marred the environment. But on a weeknight in the snow, Takaragawa's *rotenburo* can be sensational.

Ōsenkaku
Minakami-machi, Tone-gun, Gunma-ken 325-04
PHONE: 0278-75-2121   PRICE: D
TRANSPORTATION: From Jomo Kogen Station on the Joetsu Shinkan-
              sen, take the bus for 1 hour or a taxi for 40 minutes.

Yunodaira

Getting to this secluded inn means leaving your car at an unpaved parking lot, crossing a swinging bridge, and climbing up a
trail for about five minutes. A recent modernization has left
Shosenkaku somewhat nondescript, but the management is
friendly and the surroundings bucolic. The lovely *rotenburo* are a
five-minute walk down a long outdoor stairway and overlook the
Shirasuna River.

Shōsenkaku
Kuni-mura, Agatsuma-gun, Gunma-ken 377-17
PHONE: 0279-95-3221   PRICE: B
TRANSPORTATION: From Naganohara Station on the Azuma Line, take
              the bus bound for Hanashiki Onsen for 25 min-
              utes. Get off at Yunodaira Onsenguchi and walk for
              10 minutes.

Hatonoyu

This is certainly the pick of the three modest inns in this remote
enclave of separate springs. A few hundred meters off a quiet,
deep-mountain highway, Sankyuro looks tiny from the front. But
it sprawls out back and contains fully sixteen rooms. Ours was in
a sort of *hanare* (cottage) containing two rooms and a common
Western toilet and linked to the lobby by a short, covered walkway. The room was small and unremarkable but quiet. The distant baths were worth the long indoor trek. All wood, rustic, and
generous in size, they held murky, warm water that felt very good.

The water here is artificially heated. Dinner was adequate but unremarkable. Sankyuro is a laid-back, family-run place that soothes the soul.

Sankyūrō
3314 Motojuku, Agatsuma-machi, Agatsuma-gun, Gunma-ken 377-09
PHONE: 0279-69-2421   PRICE: B
TRANSPORTATION: From Gunma Haramachi Station on the Agatsuma Line, take the bus to Odo for 30 minutes. Transfer to the bus for Shimizu, ride for 25 minutes, and alight at the terminus. Walk for 5 minutes.

⟋⟋⟋

Shibahara **Onsen**

For a travel destination so close to Tokyo, Chichibu remains remarkably quaint. It's long been known for its seven *kosen* (cold-spring baths), and Shibahara is the most picturesque and off-the-beaten track of the lot. Yanagiya is one of its four inns. Physically, Yanagiya is nothing special, except for the superb soundproofing between rooms. Its rustic, earlier 130-year-old structure enhances the atmosphere but isn't used any more. On the other hand, the smallish wood and black-slate baths in the newer main building are pretty and comfortable. The artificially heated water gets awfully hot as the evening wears on but felt great around dinner-time and in the morning. The wonderful food is the best reason to come here. We gorged ourselves in our room on *tororo*; persimmon stuffed with a creamy walnut concoction; *sansai* as both tempura and *nabe*; braised trout; fried smelt; *yuzu* stuffed with grated *daikon* radish and mushrooms; raw carp more delicate than usual; steamed *konnyaku, udo*, and burdock; and the usual trimmings. We barely had room for the famous handmade *soba* we ordered ahead of time for an extra 650 yen. The owner told us everything is prepared by local farm families.

Yanagiya

2048 Shibahara, Arakawa-mura, Chichibu-gun, Saitama-ken 369-18

PHONE: 0494-54-0250   PRICE: C, D

TRANSPORTATION: From Ikebukuro, take the Seibu line's Red Arrow special express for 80 minutes to Seibu Chichibu. Walk 5 minutes to Ohanabatake Station on the Chichibu Tetsudo Line and ride 20 minutes to Bushu Hino station. Yanagiya will pick you up there.

Sengoku Shimoyu Onsen

Hakone, part of an *onsen*-strewn national park near Mount Fuji, conjures up visions of tourist hordes, traffic jams, and hotels run amok. Then there is Bangakuro. It took literally dozens of trips to Hakone before I discovered this gem of a traditional hot spring inn. On a back road between Gora and Sengokubara, only minutes from teeming towns and golf courses, rests this hushed, bucolic refuge. It's a delightful base from which to explore the undeniable attractions that bring so many visitors to Hakone.

As your taxi pulls into Bangakuro's driveway you already know it's going to be a special place. In the midst of a primeval forest, the inn has staked out several acres of tranquil gardens cascading down gentle slopes toward a tiny brook. To the right of the entryway is the original building, its thatched roof a rare sight in this part of Japan. Behind you and up a steep, stone stairway lies a compact garden replete with a miniature shrine and a teahouse. You'll be greeted by friendly, kimono-clad women who belong to the extended family that operates Bangakuro.

The sprawling, wooden, two-story structure is divided into two wings. To the left is a new section, which contains most of the costliest rooms. Down toward the right are the larger quarters and the segregated baths. Unlike most of my favorite spas, Bangakuro lacks outdoor pools. The indoor ones are small, but they're tastefully appointed in cypress and cedar and are rarely crowded since most of the guest rooms have their own private baths. You can make the men's bath co-ed without too much worry that you'll be interrupted.

Bangakuro is good value in many respects, not least of which is the abundant and delectable food. You'll be graciously served in your room with seasonal dishes ranging from hotpots to *sashimi* and wild vegetables. The rooms themselves are airy and comfortable, with the best of the lot being "Fuji no ma."

Bangakurō
1251 Sengokubara, Hakone-machi, Kanagawa-ken, 250-06
PHONE: 0460-4-8588 PRICE: D
TRANSPORTATION: Travel 15 minutes by taxi from Gora terminal on the Hakone Tozan Line, accessible from Odawara or Hakone Yumoto.
BY CAR: From the Hakone I. C. of the Odawara-Atsugi Doro, take Route 138 for about 15 kilometers. Turn left onto the local road to Sengokubara and drive for 3 kilometers.

Ashinoyu
After Bangakuro (above), this is perhaps the best choice in over-developed Hakone. And it's a convenient three kilometers to Hakone-machi on Lake Ashi. The owner of this traditional, rambling inn is considered one of Japan's premier *onsen* masters. The garden-like setting is commodious and quiet, the traditional rooms terrific and the meals sumptuous. All for a reasonable price. The very hot baths, however, are incongruously done up in charmless tile.

Matsuzakaya
55 Ashinoyu, Hakone-machi, Ashigara Shimo-gun, Kanagawa-ken 250-05
PHONE: 0460-3-6315 PRICE: C, D
TRANSPORTATION: From Odawara Station on the Tokaido and Odakyu lines, ride 50 minutes on the bus bound for Hakone-machi. Get off at Ashinoyu.

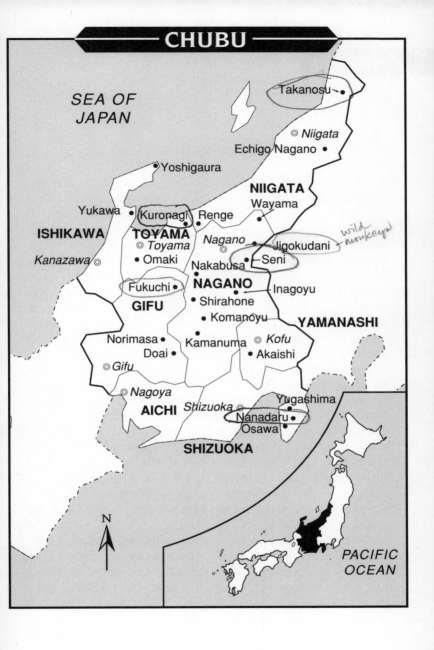

Takanosu Onsen

For its combination of luxury, traditional atmosphere, and cuisine, this unique establishment ranks right at the top with Seni and Fukuchi's Yumoto Choza. What sets Kikuya apart from the other two is its setting in a hushed compound comprising not only a restrained main building but also about a dozen private cottages scattered over a tranquil, verdant site. Though only a few years old, each of these *hanare* is rendered in superbly traditional style. Each cottage features its own indoor bath and private *rotenburo*, separate and large living and sleeping areas floored with tatami mats, Western-style toilet, and a carpeted sitting room. You can't do any better than this for privacy and serenity.

From the parking lot just off busy Route 113, traverse the swinging bridge across the Arakawa river and you'll find yourself in front of this spring's other inn, Takanosukan. Keep going and soon you'll enter Kikuya's tranquil precinct. The first building on the right houses the front desk. From here, after checking in, you'll be escorted to your very own cottage. When making your reservation, take the cheapest option. The pricier choices are more luxurious and generally face the river, but they're a bit noisy because of the road running along the opposite bank and not worth the extra money. We were blissfully content with the cottage called "Matsu."

Our cheerful maid, Sachie-san, was a delight. She anticipated our every need and personally served us the *sansai-ryori* dinner for which Kikuya prides itself. Among the gastronomical delicacies she proffered were such wild vegetables as *mizu* and *akebi*,

1. Yamadakan at Tashiro Motoyu, Aomori Pref. p 26

2. Aoni Onsen Ryokan at Aoni, Aomori Pref.

p. 27

3. Chojukan at Hoshi, Gunma Pref.

4. Inside Chojukan.

5. Kaya no Ie at Hotaka Onsen, Gunma Pref.

6. Kajika-an at Nanadaru, Shizuoka Pref. P121

P.113

7, 8. Yumoto Choza at Fukuchi Onsen, Gifu Pref.

9. Yumoto Choza at Fukuchi Onsen, Gifu Pref.

10. Gajoen at Myoken, Kagoshima Pref.

11. Yamaguchi Ryokan at Tarutama Onsen, Kumamoto Pref.

12. Inside Seifuso.

13. Seifuso at Jigoku, Kumamoto Pref.

which have no good English-language equivalents. The delicate tempura included maple leaves, chrysanthemum flowers, wild fungi, and prawn, all dipped in salt or powdered green tea. This was followed by a subtle *mazegohan* (flavored rice cooked with mixed vegetables), superb *sashimi*, interesting stuffed *mochi* (rice cakes), and the regular trimmings.

In addition to your own supremely romantic, private bath you have the option of visiting one of Kikuya's two common *rotenburo*. They're sexually segregated and exquisite. Atypically, the women's beam-roofed side exceeds the men's more modest but elegant rendition. Takanosu's water is crystal clear, odorless, hot and inviting. We dipped a lot.

Consistent with its laid-back style, the Kikuya management let us sleep in and have breakfast at 8:30; it could have even been 9:00 except for our need to hit the road. Dinner hours are also unusually flexible.

This corner of Niigata-ken is so close to Yamagata-ken that Sachie-san talked about the style of food as if it were from the latter. Looking at a map, one notes a proliferation of springs in the area. But take my word for it: Takanosu Onsent is the only one to visit.

Kikuya Ryokan
1076 Yuzawa, Sekigawa-mura, Niigata-ken 959-32
PHONE: 0254-64-1001   PRICE: D
TRANSPORTATION: From Echigo Shimoseki Station on the Yonezaka Line, the bus to Takanosu Onsen takes 15 minutes.
BY CAR: Turn east off Route 7 north of Niigata onto Route 113 and drive about 30 minutes.

✳ ✳ ✳

Echigo Nagano Onsen

Almost until arriving at this single-inn spring you think it's going to be too close to civilization. But suddenly the town recedes and you're in lush, rolling country. If you are in your own vehicle, turn right and exit off Highway 289 just before the inn and approach it from the back. This takes you down a steep hill to the to the inn's rear parking lot.

Cross the swinging bridge into isolated Rankeiso's broad, quiet compound and feast your eyes on the vast garden replete with water wheel, thatch-roofed charcoal kiln, thatched tea pavilion and carp pond. Beyond lies Rankeiso's stately original structure, dating back to 1927. The three-story wooden building has been beautifully preserved.

Once in the lobby, you may be taken aback by the incongruous hotel-like ambiance, complete with uniformed staff, carpeting, and an elevator. The furnishings are alarmingly chintz. But don't despair. Assuming you've reserved room 1315 on a corner of the original third floor, you'll be happy. It's consummately traditional and spacious, affording fine views over the garden and stream.

Located behind and connected to the old building is a tasteful but somewhat Westernized new wing that features such disarming touches as miniature gardens in the hallways, soft lighting and nicely appointed, blond-wood guest rooms with traditional tatami flooring.

It was in one of these that we were served dinner by a reserved yet disarming forty-something maid. The generally unremarkable meal was nonetheless satisfying and exquisitely presented. It included a nice *dobin-nabe* (light stew), raw carp, and beef fillet broiled on sizzling stone. The exotic-minded can also order a rare stew of *tanuki*, or raccoon dog. We had breakfast in the same room.

Rankeiso's bright and sizable indoor baths are done up in subtle, stylish tile. Artificially heated, the salty water is clear and comfortable. Excellent showers around the fringes afforded us great shampoos. The adjacent, smallish men's *rotenburo* was pleasantly rocky but marred by a noisy drain. That's presumably been fixed by now.

All in all, you can't do much better for such a relatively accessible place.

Rankeisō
Nagano, Shimoda-mura, Minami Gamahara-gun, Niigata-ken
955-01
PHONE: 0256-47-2211   PRICE: C
TRANSPORTATION: From Higashi-Sanjo Station on the Shinetsu Line,
the bus to Yagimae takes 40 minutes. The Rankeiso
bus will pick you up there.
BY CAR: From Sanjo-Tsubame I. C. on the Hokuriku Jido-
shado, take Route 289 for about 20 kilometers to
Yagi. Turn right and go about 2 kilometers.

Renge Onsen

At 1,275 meters, this is one of Japan's highest *onsen*. It sits supremely alone in majestic natural surroundings at the end of a long and twisting road boasting early autumn-tinted vistas. Beautifully maintained, the sturdy, dark-wood, lodge-like structure dates back to just 1978, when the road was finished. Before then, more basic facilities served mainly hikers. Unfortunately, management insists on retaining backpacker values despite its increasingly genteel clientele. I've never stayed in a room more fit for a monk. No table or *zabuton*, no mirror, cups, towels, or *yukata*. Just four bare walls and six tatami mats. We felt lucky to find futon in the closet. The meals are equally sparse. Given the charge of 9,000 yen per person, I've almost never been housed or fed more austerely at an *onsen*, including ones more inaccessible than this. (Only Nagano's Honzawa was worse, and with no redeeming features.) Loudspeaker blasts regularly shatter your reveries; the breakfast announcements shock you incessantly from roughly 6:50 A.M. The electricity is cut at 9 P.M. If you don't have your own form of illumination, be ready to hit the sack. Renge's saving graces are its marvelous setting and memorable baths. The indoor tubs are rustically wooden, dimly lit, and brimming with sulfuresque, translucent water of top quality. Ten minutes up a rugged, strenuous trail lie three widely scattered and tiny *rotenburo* affording wild, panoramic views. If you're a backpacker, this is a great jumping-off point for some of the best trails in the southern Japan Alps.

Hakubadake Renge Onsen
Honmachi, Itoigawa-shi, Niigata-ken 941
PHONE: 0255-52-8000   PRICE: B
TRANSPORTATION: From Hiraiwa Station on the Oito Line, the one bus a day to Renge takes 85 minutes. (Closed during the winter.)

Yoshigaura Onsen

Seaside *onsen* usually turn me off because they're almost invariably near busy roads and tacky towns. This unique establishment is a rare exception. Though flawed, it was well worth the several-hour drive up to the very tip of the remote and alluring Noto Peninsula.

Once you've reached the parking lot overlooking Ranpu no Yado, the view is breathtaking. You'll immediately espy the snug inn huddling in a rocky cove about thirty meters below, smack against the crashing surf. There's not another sign of civilization in sight. "Japan meets Maine," uttered my awestruck Canadian companion.

Five minutes later you're at the door of an inn dating back 400 years. Many of its original pillars and beams remain. Although renovated several times over the years, Ranpu no Yado retains most of the aura of ancient times. It bespeaks understated, dark-wood elegance. Throughout the inn you'll find many captivating touches: fine *kaidan dansu* (stairways that double as chests of drawers), an *irori* sitting area just off the *genkan*, polished wooden floors, and indirect lighting almost everywhere. Warmly welcomed by the owner's young wife, we were escorted to our second-floor quarters at the end of a narrow, dim corridor. The eight-mat room faced the ocean and boasted superbly decorative shoji and woodwork.

Soon it was off to the bath before dinner. Since Ranpu no Yado has only one *rotenburo*, men and women take turns. We were pleased with the softly lit, moderately sized indoor bath, clad darkly in stone and tile. Heavy, sliding-glass doors face the ocean. A sign urges bathers to shut the doors when leaving at night to keep out the occasional weasel and *tanuki* (raccoon dog).

After dinner, we sampled the unusual, roofed *rotenburo*. Dramatically perched above wave-crashed rocks, it's sheltered by artificial boulders made of fiberglass. Synthetic goes against my grain, but this is pulled off remarkably well. On the roof of the small pool is an inviting deck where you can chill out between dips.

Dinner here is a major event that took us a full hour to negotiate. The centerpiece is an enormous local crab. It was surrounded by fourteen other dishes, not including rice and soup. These included *katsuo sashimi* (sliced, raw bonito), *ama-ebi* (sweet shrimp), scallops like I've never tasted, squid with *mikan* sauce, and sea urchin. We also enjoyed stuffed baby squid, wild vegetables, broiled fish, burdock wrapped in fish, prawn wrapped in lotus root, and on and on. This meal alone in Tokyo would have cost as much as our entire stay here.

As mentioned earlier, Ranpu no Yado is flawed. For one thing, although it widely advertises itself as illuminated by kerosene lamps (*ranpu* means "lamp"), these turn out to be a mere contrivance. Four brand-new cottages line the entrance up to the main inn. Thankfully, they're done in superb traditional style and would be worth staying in for the small premium. Unfortunately, they front an egregious, bright-blue swimming pool. Still, this is a journey worth making.

Ranpu no Yado
Noroshi, Misaki-machi, Suzu-shi, Ishikawa-ken 927-14
PHONE: 0768-86-2136   PRICE: C, D
TRANSPORTATION: From Suzu Station on the Noto Line, take the bus for Kinoura by way of Noroshi for 50 minutes to Yoshigaura. Walk for 15 minutes.
BY CAR: From Kanazawa-higashi I. C. on the Hokuriku Expressway, take Routes 159 and 249 to Suzu. Then

drive about 15 kilometers on local road No. 28 to the sign.

Yukawa Onsen

This humdrum inn, whose name amusingly means "Pavilion of the Dragon King," gets my vote mainly for its location. Situated on one of the loveliest back roads I've traversed in Japan, it could be a convenient stop for travelers on the way up the Noto Peninsula. Ryuokaku mainly serves a clientele of local farmers. All the better for authenticity. And the baths, while utilitarian, offer up unusually hard, red-brown, iron-scented water. My Canadian companion thought this and the heavenly surroundings alone qualified Ryuokaku for an entry in this guide. While his points are well-taken, I wouldn't necessarily recommend staying here. But for a taste of irrepressibly unspoiled Noto, you can't do better for a drop-in.

Ryūōkaku
35-7, 47 Bu, Yukawa-machi, Nanao-shi, Ishikawa-ken 926
PHONE: 0767-58-1117   PRICE: A
TRANSPORTATION: From Nanao Station on the Nanao Line, the bus takes 40 minutes.

Wayama Onsen

At the inner reaches of fabled Nakatsugawa Gorge spanning Gifu and Nagano prefectures, Wayama serves up some of the finest *onsen* scenery going. And that's after an hour-long drive through splendid mountain country remarkably unspoiled for an area as well-known as this. You'll pass several springs along the way, best of which for a drop-in is Sakasamaki Onsen, while you're still in Gifu.

Once you've reached Wayama's enclave the string of humdrum *minshuku* may put you off. Forge ahead, following the signs, and soon you'll be at road's end. Here lies resplendently isolated Jinseikan in a redoubt to where the defeated Taira clan fled and hid from the central government in the twelfth century in one of Japan's most enduringly sentimental sagas.

The inn itself isn't much to behold from the outside. The inside is rather mundane as well. Rooms are small, pedestrian, and poorly soundproofed. There are some appealing touches, to be sure, such as the parquet entryway.

Best of all is the *rotenburo*, which on first glance looks somewhat ordinary. But soon after entering the half-sheltered, mixed-bathing pools, satisfaction starts to run deep. The clear, perfect-temperature water is infused with *yunohana*, the bits of sulfur and other particulates found in occasional *onsen* baths. Even some Japanese are put off by this, but true connoisseurs regard *yunohana* as the mark of a fine spring. Then there's the magnificent view over a distant river toward majestic cliffs on the other side. In mid-October the autumn tints were most excellent.

Another highlight was dinner, notwithstanding the utilitarian *shokudo* in which it was served. Courses ran the gamut from mountain vegetables such as *fuki*, *maitake*, wild mushrooms in *tororo*, and special bamboo shoots, to foil-baked chicken with butter, *enokidake* and green onions, crab *nabe*, and broiled rock-fish. Each course was explained in detail to the dozen or so diners by Mrs. Sekiya, the proprietress. She described how she and her husband gathered the various ingredients from local forests and explained the special properties of each. This became somewhat didactic after a while, but the Japanese clientele seemed to eat it up, so to speak. Then, toward meal's end, Mr. and Mrs. Sekiya entertained the assemblage with a couple of local folk songs. This could have seemed corny but, as the Sekiya's intentions were genuine, proved touching.

To further spruce up your dinner, pre-order *kotsuzake* as soon as you arrive. This is whole rockfish simmered in saké and served in a largish bowl with lots of the hot rice wine. It's a rarely found delicacy of certain mountain inns and well worth a try. Remember that this is an unusual dish and you'll need to order it a couple of hours before mealtime.

Jinseikan

Wayama, Sakae-mura, Shimominochi, Nagano-ken
PHONE: 0257-67-2205   PRICE: B
TRANSPORTATION: From Echigo Yuzawa on the Joetsu Shinkansen, the bus for Morimiyanohara or Nozawa Onsen to Tsunan takes about 50 minutes. Change at Tsunan for the bus to Wayama Onsen and ride for 80 minutes.
BY CAR: From Tsunan-machi on Route 117, head south on Route 405 for about 28 kilometers. Turn right at the sign.

Jigokudani ~~TOO FAR TO WALK~~

Better known and more frequented than many of the other *onsen* in this guide, Jigokudani, and its single inn get my nod anyway for uniqueness, authenticity, and value. Unique is the prevalence of wild monkeys. They don't enter the *rotenburo* with you, as many people mistakenly believe. Instead, they have their own outdoor pool about a five-minute walk from Korakukan. If you visit at about 8:30 A.M., you're virtually guaranteed the unforgettable sight of primates venturing out of the forest to bathe and preen. This attraction comes at no additional cost and is remarkably non-commercialized.

Korakukan's authenticity is accentuated by its location, just a couple of kilometers from some of the most hideous *onsen* development in Japan. The nearby bathing towns of Yudanaka and Shibu are so horrific as to make the likes of Kusatsu and Atami seem heavenly. But get yourself to one of the two parking lots from which trails to Jigokudani depart and you're on your way to amazingly proximate tranquillity. The only way in is by foot and you'll need to walk ten to thirty minutes depending on where you park or get off the bus.

Wooden Korakukan sprawls over a small escarpment just above a stony river bed. No aesthetic gem, to be sure, but the real thing. Inside you'll find the steep staircases and narrow, wood-planked corridors characteristic of ancient inns. All marvelously rustic but clean. Our room, infelicitously dubbed No. 88, was roomy, quiet, simple, and probably one of the best in the house. It lacked its own facilities but, for 10,000 yen a head in such a popular place, we were content.

Dinner confirmed that this place is a good value. We enjoyed surprisingly good sashimi for such an inland redoubt, a rich duck *nabe*, grilled rice balls, and all the normal trimmings. This was served in a pleasant, tatami *shokudo* (dining hall) in a separate building just across from the *genkan*.

Korakukan's simple, wooden, indoor baths are ___ hottest I've experienced. Their water spurts out of th ___ 70–80 degrees Centigrade (the gurgling spring-head ___ cated and easily visible just across the stream). U_ *onsen*, the management here makes no effort to cool th___ you'll want to run lots of cold water yourself. Better yet, head for the sometimes convivial mixed-bathing *kon'yoku rotenburo*. It's just the right temperature. Unfortunately, it's also exposed to daytrippers so go after dark or in the pre-breakfast hours.

As I've indicated, Jigokudani gets lots of daytime visitors, most of whom don't get to see the famous monkeys unless they know to arrive at around 8:30 A.M. The nights here are tranquil, though. You'll pinch yourself at the thought you're so close to egregious civilization.

Kōrakukan

Yamanouchi-cho, Shimotakai-gun, Nagano-ken 381-04
PHONE: 0269-33-4376   PRICE: B
TRANSPORTATION: From Yudanaka Station on the Nagano Dentetsu line, take the bus to Kamibayashi Onsen for 15 minutes. Then walk for 30 minutes.
BY CAR: From Route 403 south of Iiyama City, take Route 292 toward Shiga Heights. After about 4 kilometers, turn left toward Yudanaka and Shibu. Follow the signs to the Jigokudani parking lot and walk for 15 minutes.

* * *

Seni Onsen

GOOD

Anyone but a purist would put this wonderful inn at the very top of the *onsen* scale. I rank it third overall only because it's not as primitively evocative as a couple of others. But for sheer Epicurean delight in a remarkably tasteful renovation, Iwanoyu goes unrivaled. It's also an unbelievable bargain.

Your first taste of Iwanoyu's specialness comes as you pass through the traditional, covered gate leading from the parking lot into the inn's precincts. There you'll find a cozy sitting area replete with a hot-embered hibachi and elegant artwork. Proceeding along the stony path, you'll soon come to the *genkan*, where the welcome is as genuinely warm as at any inn I've visited. A kimono-clad maid will guide you to the rustic tea-room just off the small lobby. Here she will ply you with a relaxing cup of salty *umecha* (plum tea) while you fill out the registration form. Then she'll escort you to your room, which is guaranteed to be as pleasant as any you've ever experienced.

Next you'll want to head for the bath, of course. And Iwanoyu's is truly unique. It comprises a large cave up against which the inn is built. Split into a V-shaped configuration, it's an amateur spelunker's dream come true. Veering along the right-hand side of the V you can ascend past several ethereally illuminated pools to the very end of the cave, which is almost completely dark. Even on a Saturday night we encountered few other bathers. The mineral-infused water is barely above room temperature, which, along with the adventuresome setting, makes this a terrific choice for families with young children unused to scalding baths. But for those seeking a proper hot soak Iwanoyu offers small, elegant tubs on both the men's and women's sides that adjoin the mixed-bathing cave pools. All in all this is one of the most exhilarating bathing experiences in Japan.

After your early evening bath you'll be ready for dinner, and Iwanoyu's is unrivaled for the price. Following the maid's directions you'll wend your way to the romantically lit dining area, which resembles a tiny, enclosed hamlet comprising about ten private, tatami-floored pavilions under a common roof. Rarely have I felt a stronger sense of sublime, traditional Japan. And the food lives up to the atmosphere. Relying strictly on local ingredients, the chef conjures up a menu of astonishing quality, quantity, and imagination, impeccably served. Breakfast is equally sumptuous. For the same dining experience in Tokyo you would pay the entire cost of a night at Iwanoyu.

Iwanoyu
Seni Onsen, Susaka-shi, Nagano-ken 382
PHONE: 0262-45-2453   PRICE: D
TRANSPORTATION: From Tokyo, take the Shinetsu Line from Ueno to Nagano, then transfer to the Nagano Dentetsu Line. After a 25-minute ride to Susaka, take the Seni-bound bus for 30 minutes. You can get off at Ueda before Nagano, and drive by rental car over the scenic Sugadaira Heights.

taxi?

BY CAR: From Susaka I. C. on the Nagano Expressway, take local road No. 30 for 4.5 kilometers to Route 406. Turn left and drive about 9 kilometers.

✳ ✳ ✳

Nakabusa Onsen

_No_

My friend Robin Berrington, an American diplomat and _onsen_ aficionado nonpareil, calls this the "Disneyland of _Onsen_." He's close, and in the best sense. There's little contrivance at Nakabusa. What you've got instead is an enormous complex of disparate, mostly traditional buildings belonging to one inn that can house 300 people and often do. Scattered throughout are, count them, twelve different baths, indoors and out, offering three kinds of water. That doesn't include the separate men's and women's sections. So mind-boggling is the complexity of it all that you're handed a map when you arrive.

Then there are the crowds. The lobby is like a train station. We had to wait about ten minutes for our turn to be guided to our room. Don't let this put you off, though. After about thirty minutes of roaming around, everything comes into synch. And once in your room, tranquillity happens.

One reaches remote Nakabusa after negotiating a tortuous, twenty-kilometer drive up to 1,400 meters and the base of trails leading into the northern Japan Alps. This is an ancient *onsen* in serious mountainscape.

You make this effort less for comfort, serenity, and fine dining than for the baths and the scene. Our room, though ostensibly one of the better ones in the house, was perfectly acceptable but mundane. Dinner was bountiful but unexceptional—raw carp, rockfish marinated in *miso* and broiled in *sasa* (bamboo grass), duck stew, *soba*, etc.

So maximize your time in the baths. To save you futile exploring, here's an easy guide. By far the best indoor pool is "Furo-no-Yu." Though new, it's one of the most romantic bathhouses in all of Japan. Built of treasured and fragrant *hinoki* throughout, including large ceiling beams, this is a serene, immaculate respite from the rest of bustling Nakabusa. The largish, mixed-bathing tub is lined with sophisticated dark slate and bedecked with small boulders that extend through a small opening to the outside. The water is divine.

Of the seven *rotenburo*, roofed "Shirotaki no Yu" stands out. At the far upper-right-hand corner of the complex, it's rustic and isolated. That does not mean unpopular. We encountered many bathers here of both sexes. The two adjacent mixed-bathing tubs can comfortably accommodate eight or so bathers. Also worth checking out is "Oza no Yu," the original bath of this *onsen*. Small, wooden, and funky, it's housed in the ancient wooden quarters that date back to the Meiji-era days when famed British explorer Walter Weston stayed here. It was he who discovered Kamikochi and gave the Japan Alps their name.

Nakabusa Onsen Ryokan
Ariake, Hotaka-machi, Minami Azumi-gun, Nagano-ken 399-83
PHONE: 0263-35-9704   PRICE: B, C, D
TRANSPORTATION: From Hotaka Station on the Oito Line, the bus to
                Nakabusa Onsen takes 70 minutes. (The bus runs

only during Golden Week, summer, and fall.) Otherwise, a taxi from Ariake Station takes 40 minutes.

BY CAR: From Route 147 north of Matsumoto, turn west at Ariake, and follow the signs to Nakabusa for about 21 kilometers.

✳ ✳ ✳

Shirahone Onsen   No

This redoubt of scattered, tranquil *onsen* inns is a spring-lover's paradise. Shirahone's sulfurous, bluish-gray water is among Japan's finest. And the rugged, verdant surroundings refresh the soul. We loved trying the various baths, searching out the wee noodle shop at the top of the hill, and soaking up the scenery.

Sprawling Motoyu Saito, the descendant of Shirahone's original establishment, is the place to stay although it could be so much better. The enchanting lobby is done up in dark wood and indirectly illuminated through shoji panels in the low ceilings. To the right is a small *irori* (sunken hearth) lounge and a cozy coffee corner. The three traditional wings are well preserved and attractive. Not only are vending machines well hidden, but pretty gravel mini-gardens, urns, and flower arrangements grace hallway corners.

The three indoor baths, unstintingly *hinoki* throughout, are small but pleasing. The best and biggest is "Ryujin no Yu" on the top floor of the *honkan* (main wing), which is where I would recommend staying. Basically for men, it's reserved for women from 6–9 P.M. The naturally hot water in all three baths was just the right temperature. The two mixed-bathing *rotenburo*, one with a roof, lie next to each other along an outdoor stairway detached from the inn. They're pleasant enough but in winter one was closed and the other not quite hot enough.

Indeed, the *rotenburo* symbolizes Motoyu Saito's somewhat careless management. The one pool open in winter was too shallow and had barbed wire on one side. Exposed pipes detracted from the otherwise pretty setting. Inside the inn, carpets are frayed and stained; unused furniture, supplies and bric-a-brac are stuck in crannies within plain view.

Dinner, served in a rustic dining room, was mediocre at best, save for a succulent duck stew. The *chawanmushi* was flavorless, the marinated *ayu* revolting, the cold noodles insipid.

Our six-tatami-mat room was basic, with a cramped sitting area and no toilet. At least the futons were extra thick and the inn very restful at night despite the many guests.

We'd have focused less on the faults if we'd been paying less. Shirahone in general is overpriced and Motoyu Saito offers only two room-and-meal packages, one fully 77 percent more expensive than the other. We opted for the cheaper alternative because the more expensive one was beyond my 20,000-yen ceiling. A look at the newer rooms convinced me they weren't worth it.

But Shirahone's other inns are even more seriously flawed. So come here for the baths and environment. Spend more time in the lovely lounge area than in your room and bring lots of snacks.

Motoyu Saitō Ryokan
Azumi-mura, Azumi-gun, Nagano-ken 390-15
PHONE: 0263-93-2311   PRICE: C
TRANSPORTATION: From Matsumoto Station on the Chuo Line, take the Matsumoto Dentetsu Line for 30 minutes to Niijima Station. From there, the bus to Shirahone Onsen takes about 70 minutes.
BY CAR: From Matsumoto I. C. on the Chuo Expressway, take Route 158 for about 34 kilometers. Turn left at the sign and drive about 5 kilometers. (In winter, turn left at Nagawato, 27 kilometers from the expressway. Take local road No. 26 for 6.5 kilometers to Nagawa. Turn left onto the Kamikochi-Norikura Rindo for 22 kilometers.)

✳   ✳   ✳

Kamanuma Onsen

I showed up at this small, out-of-the-way inn without a reservation on a snowy, late-December weekday but was politely turned away because it was closed for annual pre-New Year's cleaning. This was the third place that day with the same story. Daikisen's rustic-lodge appearance, snug lobby, and bucolic location looked so enticing, though, that I made a point of going back a couple of months later to check it out. I'm glad I did.

The *hinoki genkan* and pine-paneled lounge were just as charming as my earlier glimpse had suggested. The air was delicately perfumed by the wood-burning stove, and flowers were everywhere. The entire decor was tasteful and homey. We received a warm welcome at the tiny front desk from the woman who had turned me away two months before. She called upon her husband, Mr. Taguchi, to show us to our room.

Mr. Taguchi, a very young sixty years old at the time, comes from this rugged, relatively unpopulated area but had worked in Tokyo for years as a "salaryman." In the early 1980s he got fed up and returned to convert the lonely *minshuku* his father had built into an inn.

For a place aimed at the economy-minded, Taguchi-san got almost everything right. The single-story guest wing is concrete, for example, but he's covered the front with dark wood. Our room, No. 10, was at the end of the hall and faced the stream to the back. A plain eight mats, it was spanking clean and well heated. Pristine toilets and sinks were just down the hall. But why spend much time here when the lounge and baths beckon?

The latter are two accommodating, segregated, *hinoki* tubs of good size. Called *"rotenburo,"* they're actually covered in greenhouse-style vinyl. Only the far end opens, and then only in summer. This is my only real quibble with Daikisen. But the murky, greenish-brown water felt so good in the wood that I probably took more baths here than anyplace. And that's despite the baths' early closing at 9:00 P.M. and early the checkout time of 9:00 A.M.

Dinner here is another highlight. Home-made, mainly by Mr. Taguchi, it was innovative and served in a pleasant, tatami-floored *shokudo*. We happily chewed our way through grilled rock-fish; raw horsemeat; *sobazushi*; tofu covered with a sweet *miso* paste; duck, mushrooms, and other goodies grilled on a leaf; skewered meatballs studded with raw green *soba*; baked potato; tempura of ginseng and *sansai* (mountain vegetables); *gomadofu* with a tangy lemon and miso sauce; a bowl of unusual black rice; and all the trimmings.

Mr. Taguchi has built a huge log house out back that he lets out to groups of at least six to eight at a premium. It boasts its own beautiful bath and lots of lovely features, but you eat in the inn's dining room with the other guests.

People say nearby Haizawa Onsen is worth checking out. I tried twice, but Haizawa was closed on both occasions.

Daikisen
Midake-mura, Kiso-gun, Nagano-ken
PHONE: 0264-46-2155   PRICE: B,
                                       C for the log house
TRANSPORTATION: From Kiso Fukushima Station on the Chuo Line, the bus bound for Ropeway takes about 20 minutes. Get off at Tokiwabashi, walk back across the bridge, and take the road to the right for 15 minutes. A taxi from the station takes 20 minutes.
BY CAR: From Route 19 south of Kiso Fukushima, turn left at Torii and drive about 4 kilometers. Turn left just before Tokiwabashi for 1 kilometer.

───────────── ♨ ─────────────

Inagoyu Onsen
Snuggled in a larch forest 1,500 meters high, this log-cabin style,

secluded inn is a favorite among backpackers. But it's much more comfortable and civilized than your typical climbers' lodge. The rooms are spick-and-span and reasonably appointed. The segregated baths are roomy and attractive, with naturally fizzy water.

Inagoyu Ryokan
1343 Inago, Koumi-machi, Minami Saku-gun, Nagano-ken 384-11
PHONE: 0267-93-2262   PRICE: B
TRANSPORTATION: From Koumi Station on the Koumi Line, the bus to Inagoyu takes 45 minutes. In winter, the inn will pick you up.

Komanoyu Onsen

On a snowy afternoon in late December, after trying several inns in the general vicinity that all turned out to be closed for their annual pre-holiday cleaning, I was relieved to finally be embraced by the warm hospitality of this stately inn. Only three kilometers from the bustling town of Kiso Fukushima, Komanoyu Ryokan resides alone off a little-trafficked mountain road. The best room in the house is "Komagatake," followed closely by "Hotaka," where I stayed. It amounted to a comfortable, standard eight-tatami-mat room with a carpeted sitting area overlooking a garden with a pretty pool, a man-made waterfall, cute footbridge, and a waterwheel. The room also included a private Japanese toilet, sink, and wooden mini-bath. Much better were the inn's two artificially heated main baths. One, in a cellar-like setting, offered up reddish-brown water of obviously ample mineral content. The other, supposedly more famous bath, boasted crystal-clear, odorless water infused with the essences of a number of medicinal plants. Dinner, served in the room, was basically par for the course except for a notable succulent cut of braised pork with green onions and a memorable morsel of duck steamed in a leaf.

Komanoyu Ryokan
47-2 Kiso Fukushima-machi, Nagano-ken 397
PHONE: 0264-23-2288 PRICE: B, C
TRANSPORTATION: From Kiso Fukushima on the Chuo Line, a taxi or the inn minibus takes 15 minutes.

Kuronagi Onsen   ~~TOO FAR~~

Of the five reasonably accessible springs in the famous Kurobe Gorge, this is the clear choice. And even though it's the closest, getting there is still half the fun.

From nightmarishly developed Unazuki Onsen you board the miniature Kurobe Keikoku Tetsudo train that climbs and winds for almost two hours into the furthest reaches of the gorge. When I took this delightful ride for the first time in 1980, the little train had few passengers and Kurobe was still relatively unspoiled. When I went back in late 1993, I found the train mobbed with tour groups and the gorge a beehive of hideous road, bridge, and dam development.

But the ride is still quaint and fun, especially if you avoid going on packed-out weekends and the high season. When buying tickets you'll face a confusion of four different prices, each for a different grade of coach. Unless it's raining, opt for the cheapest, which gives you a no-frills, open-air car. Otherwise, buy the next-cheapest. The two more expensive alternatives offer unnecessary comfort. Anyway, it's only a twenty-five-minute ride to Kuronagi. When you get off, you'll find a sign for the inn pointing up a steep, stone staircase. Actually, that's the long way. Instead, enter the illuminated tunnel that heads left from the front end of the train and follow the utility tracks for several hundred meters until you see a sign pointing down a narrower tunnel to the right. Descend for another couple-hundred meters and turn right as soon as you exit the tunnel. Soon you'll be at Kuronagi's front door.

You're now at a truly hidden spring, and a funky one to boot, in its own private, subsidiary gorge. The ramshackle inn, which tumbles down the gorge, is larger than the modest entryway at the top would suggest. Don't look for creature comforts here—the *senmenjo* (washing area) is open-air and the quarters are extremely Spartan—but there's real atmosphere. Ask for Room 28, which is at the end of the hall and faces the heavenly stream and a long, narrow waterfall.

The indoor baths are a bit dank and utilitarian but boast good, clear water. A major highlight is the large, boulder-strewn *rotenburo* about a three-minute walk from the *genkan*. It's as wildly natural as any outdoor bath I've enjoyed.

The meals here are typical and basic—broiled *iwana* (rockfish), simple *sashimi*, and tempura—and eaten in a prosaic common area. To spruce up your meal, pre-order *kotsuzake*, a large bowl of hot saké and whole *iwana*. Pass it around for delectable sips.

Kuronagi requires a deposit that you must not fail to send in advance. We were almost rejected because I forgot.

Kuronagi Onsen
Unazuki, Toyama-ken 938-02
PHONE: 0765-62-1802   PRICE: A
TRANSPORTATION: From Unazuki Station on the Toyama Chiho Tetsudo Line, walk to the Kurobe Keikoku Tetsudo Station and ride 25 minutes to Kuronagi. Walk for about 10 minutes.
BY CAR: From Kurobe I. C. on the Hokuriku Jidoshado, drive 12 kilometers to Unazuki. Board the train there.

* * *

 # Ōmaki Onsen

Even more than Kuronagi in the same prefecture, getting here is a major part of the experience: the only way in and out is by river boat. From Komaki Dam on national route 156 you board a boat that can carry several dozen passengers and head south on the deep and tranquil Sho River for about thirty minutes until you reach the inn. The ride isn't spectacularly scenic, but soon after departure you're in a deep, leafy mountain gorge despoiled only intermittently by small power works. Eventually, the road high above to the right disappears.

After this, the inn has to be gimmicky or a rip-off, right? Not so. It turns out to be a large, traditional, conscientious establishment with few pretensions. Built smack against the river deep in the heart of nature, it seemingly goes on forever. Each of the three wings boasts its own identity and a wide array of room styles. All things considered, after investigating the quarters in all three, I would opt for the *shinkan*, or new wing, which lies in the middle. That happens to be where we stayed and we were quite happy with our room, "Hana." On the second floor, it offered a superb river view. We watched a magnificent hawk glide gracefully as close as a meter away from our window. Very quiet, "Hana's" eight tatami mats, Persian-style carpet, sitting area overlooking the river, and large entryway with sink and Western-style toilet made for a comfortable stay. Our maid was lively and solicitous. Be sure to tip yours 2,000 yen.

While generally well-maintained and bright, Omaki is a bit rough around the edges. Hallway walls are scarred and our room's windows weren't very clean. Worse yet, they inexplicably lacked screens in what is very buggy territory. Omaki also caters to tour groups, which can be noisy. But if you specify a second-floor room in the *shinkan*, you'll be spared most of that.

The baths turned out to be slightly disappointing. The largish indoor pools take only partial advantage of the river setting on which they front. The mixed-bathing but essentially men-only main *rotenburo* sits out back, with no view. But it's commodious, nicely laid-out, and comfortable. A women's *rotenburo* rests on an outdoor stair-climb above the men's.

Dinner, served in our room, turned out to be a feast of both raw and deep-fried stuffed crab legs, steak, *mazegohan* (flavored rice cooked with mixed vegetables), *sashimi* (sliced, raw fish), duck stew, mountain vegetables, and on and on. Not the best

cooking in the world but satisfying nonetheless. For breakfast w
went to the large tatami-floored *shokudo* (dining room) and sat
around an *irori* where dried *aji* (horse mackerel) were grilled.

Ōmaki Onsen Kankō Ryokan

44 Omaki, Toga-mura, Tonami-gun, Toyama-ken 932-03
PHONE: 0763-82-0363   PRICE: D
TRANSPORTATION: From Takaoka Station on the Hokuriku Line, the
bus bound for Shimohara takes 70 minutes. Get off
at Komaki Dam.
BY CAR: From Tonami I. C. on the Hokuriku Jidoshado, drive
11 kilometers south to Komaki Dam. Avoid the
paid parking lot near the embarkation point and
park for free right in front of the dock entrance by
the river.

Doai Onsen

Of small, deep-mountain but accessible *onsen* I've visited, Doai Onsen ranks very high for its combination of comfort, management, and authenticity. At the end of a long, demanding, often unpaved road, homey Doai makes the journey well worthwhile.

The single inn's two buildings are small and wooden. The main structure lies at the top of a steep, stone stairway. Enter the inn and you'll be greeted spontaneously by one of the very few staff members. From the outset this beautifully maintained, understated place feels right, from the polished, light-brown wooden floors and bright, airy ambiance to the *irori* dining area off the lobby. No vending machines, electronic games, or ugly souvenir shops here. No affectation, either. Call it natural and civilized.

We were soon escorted down a steep and narrow interior wooden staircase to our room in the other building, which lies next to the parking lot but lacks an obvious *genkan* from the outside. As things turned out, it would have been much smarter to have left our luggage in the car and retrieved it once settled into our room. But there are rooms in both structures so there's no way of knowing unless you inquire by telephone in advance.

Our room, "Sawara," was perfectly acceptable. Rather bare and dimly lit, it was an ample eight mats with pleasing green walls, wood ceiling, and trim. It shared a *roka* corridor with two other rooms fronting an expanse of windows affording leafy views. But the mellowness of our fellow guests mitigated any loss of privacy we might have felt. Rooms in the upper building, including "Shakunage," "Tsuta," and "Ume," are decoratively more appealing. But they may be noisier as they are closer to the bathing and dining areas.

Doai Onsen's bright baths are compact but captivating. Done up in a classy combination of wood and tile, they house tiny tubs of treasured cypress that contain excellent mineral water heated from its natural eleven degrees. Finding ourselves almost shoulder-to-shoulder in one of the small tubs, a Nagoya businessman and I wound up having a good conversation. The dressing rooms outside the baths are also lined with redolent wood.

For dinner, ask to eat in the space adjacent to the lobby. It has much more atmosphere than the regular dining area. Our satisfying dinner included raw and braised carp, a fine grilled rockfish, mushroom *nabe* (stew), sesame tofu, and gooey *mochigome* (sticky rice).

Being somewhat distant from civilization, Doai relies on a portable generator for its electricity. Until fairly recently, management provided oil lamps for illumination after about 10:00 P.M. That's unfortunately no longer the case. Lights out these days isn't until about 11:00 P.M. By that time virtually everyone's already asleep.

Doai Onsen
Doai Onsen, Tsukechi-machi, Ena-gun, Gifu-ken 508-03
PHONE: 0573-79-2222   PRICE: A
TRANSPORTATION: From Nakatsugawa Station on the Chuo Line, the bus to Doai Onsen takes 2 hours. (Bus runs only in summer.)
BY CAR: From Route 257 southeast of Gero, turn at Tsukechi-kyo and drive about 13 kilometers. Closed during the winter.

Norimasa Onsen

True to its name, Komeno Ryokan rests sedately among small rice paddies in the quiet hills above garish Gero Onsen. On a wee, peaceful road where foothill farms bump up against mountains, this authentic wooden structure beckons. The appealing, polished-wood *genkan* tells you right away how well the otherwise modest but comfortable establishment is maintained. Why the management hasn't arranged a suitably sublime bath remains a mystery. But next time a Japanese friend suggests going to famous but frightful Gero Onsen, insist on this consummately superior alternative. It's right out of the Japan I remember from thirty years ago.

Komeno Ryokan
Norimasayuya, Gero-machi, Masuda-gun, Gifu-ken
PHONE: 05762-6-3311   PRICE: B, C
TRANSPORTATION: From Gero Station on the Takayama Line, the bus
            to Norimasa Onsen takes 25 minutes.

Akaishi Onsen

Way up a demanding, nearly tortuous mountain road featuring majestic views of Mount Fuji, Akaishi huddles all alone. It was closed on my visit but I can testify that the remote setting is splendid, the inn rustic, and the *rotenburo* large. There's a barbecue-picnic area out front.

> **Akaishi Onsen**
> Hirabayashi, Masuho-cho, Yamagata-ken
> PHONE: 0556-22-5188   PRICE: B
> TRANSPORTATION: From Kajikazawaguchi Station on the Minobu Line, take the bus to Aoyanagi Shako for 10 minutes. Change to the bus bound for Hirabayashi and alight at the terminus after 20 minutes. The inn will pick you up there.

Yugashima Onsen

The Izu Peninsula must have as high a concentration of *onsen* as any district in Japan. But its proximity to Tokyo has made it a tourism mecca with all the attendant traffic jams, high prices, and over-development. One of the few surviving oases of tranquillity is Yumotokan, a favored haunt of the late Nobel Prize-winning author Yasunari Kawabata. Here he was inspired to write one of his most celebrated stories—*Izu-no-Odoriko*, or *The Izu Dancer*.

The strong-willed owner, Tamae Ando, represents the third generation of her family to run the 120-year-old spa, and has done a commendable job of resisting undue modernization. Yumotokan isn't necessarily top value. For the same money elsewhere you can get better baths, finer cuisine, and superior atmosphere. But in convenient Izu there aren't many better bets than this after Kajika-an.

Ando-san's modest establishment rests in a hollow at the foot of Yugashima, a quiet agglomeration of widely spaced inns that spill gracefully down a leafy mountainside in central Izu. The loveliest feature of Yumotokan is its lonely position next to the rushing Kano River, whose dim roar will lull even confirmed insomniacs who've arranged a room facing the stream. Better yet, the detached *rotenburo* sits just next to the Kanogawa, whose opposite steep bank is an uninterrupted expanse of foliage. In the distance hangs a swinging bridge connecting the next inn to its *rotenburo*.

Yumotokan takes pride in its food. It's one of the only places I've stayed whose freshwater *ayu* aren't farmed but are caught instead by local anglers. The difference in taste and texture is remarkable. Even more famous is the inn's *inoshishi nabe*, or wild boar stew. Again, the boar have been hunted, not raised. The stew's secret is a delectable, miso-based broth made from a secret recipe. It's part of the regular menu from October through late winter.

There are some enjoyable walks to be had from Yumotokan. Climb back up to the street running above the inn, cross it, and keep climbing the narrow road to the next hotel. Straight ahead you'll find a tree-shrouded path that winds above the river to a waterfall and beyond. At night, try venturing out clad in your *yukata* and wooden *geta*, turn left on the darkened street above Yumotokan and clack your way along perhaps 300 meters, past the next inn, to a tiny *sunakku* on the left: it's a welcoming and affordable *karaoke* bar whose mama-san is hospitably eager to please.

Ando-san is one of those inn owners who's had her share of problems with foreigners (although I've seen no others on my visits there). So when calling for reservations, you or your representative may need to exercise a bit of persuasion to the effect that you won't be a nuisance. Once you've arrived, you'll find the reception suitably welcoming.

Yumotokan

1656-1 Yugashima, Amagi Yugashima-machi, Shizuoka-ken 410-32

PHONE: 05588-5-1028   PRICE: D

TRANSPORTATION: From Mishima on the Tokaido Shinkansen, take the Izu–Hakone Railway for 35 minutes to its Shuzenji terminus. Then take a bus or taxi for 25–35 minutes to Yugashima Onsen.

BY CAR: Drive 10.5 kilometers south of Shuzenji Onsen on Routes 136 and 414, then turn at the sign and drive 1 kilometer more.

✳   ✳   ✳

Nanadaru Onsen

Few inns boast a name as evocative as this one's—Hermitage of the Singing Frogs. Fewer still live up to their name. Kajika-an does. Cloistered among soaring cedars, lush vegetation, and a rushing stream in the deepest reaches of the bustling Nanadaru Onsen enclave, cozy Kajika-an is as soothing a retreat as one could hope for anywhere, much less in development-crazed Izu.

Originally a restaurant of distinction, Kajika-an was expanded to a six-room inn just a few years ago. The renovation is sublime, resonating with a traditional, folkcraft motif. This is obvious from the moment you make your way through the unassuming entrance and encounter an iron kettle hanging over smoldering embers in the middle of the snug lobby. You've just entered a different world. Abutting the lobby are several quaint tatami-matted dining rooms, each with a Japanese *irori* (sunken hearth) in the middle. As your gracious maid, probably a member of the Tsuchiya family that owns the place, guides you to your room, you'll note that there's not a vending machine in sight.

If you've reserved wisely, you will have taken one of the three guest rooms without an *irori*. Why? Because your living quarters won't be interrupted by the serving of meals and you'll enjoy the variety of eating in one of the lovely dining areas. We appreciated, for example, being able to sleep until 8:30 A.M. without being disturbed for breakfast. Very few other inns that let us sleep so late. So goes Kajika-an's solicitousness.

All of the rooms face the inn's back yard, which is mainly consumed by an assortment of large concrete tanks in which Kajika-an raises its own fish. You'll appreciate this at dinner when you're plied with an array of *ayu* (sweetfish) and *yamame* (a kind of trout) done up in different delectable styles. Also memorable are the mountain vegetables and the wild-boar stew. It's soon obvious how Kajika-an won fame as a restaurant.

Living up to everything else are the baths. The men's and

women's indoor pools are rock-clad and comfy. Just off the men's, and accessible by a bit of deft footwork from the women's, are two compact *rotenburo* of exquisite charm. At the foot of towering cedars, they're nicely landscaped and comfortingly private. In several visits, we two couples were never disturbed. Out back, beyond the fish pools, are the main *rotenburo*. Separated by sex, small but accommodating, they look over the bubbling Kawazu River. Again, we easily integrated the empty men's bath. Kajika-an's water is clear, odorless, and just the right temperature.

Downstream, near the other inns, lie the seven small waterfalls that Nanadaru denotes. They're worth the brief stroll it will take to reach them on your way to or from Kajika-an.

Kajika-an
471-1 Nashimoto, Kawazu-machi, Kamo-gun, Shizuoka-ken 413-06
PHONE: 05583-6-8311   PRICE: D
TRANSPORTATION: From Kawazu Station on the Izu Kyuko Line, the bus for Shuzenji takes 25 minutes. Get off at Nanadaru and walk for 15 minutes.
BY CAR: From Kawazuhama on Route 135 between Shimoda and Inatori, turn west onto local route No. 14, which merges into Route 414 heading north. After about 9 kilometers turn left at the sign for Nanadaru.

Ōsawa Onsen

This remarkable inn has legions of foreign devotees, which is one reason it's not a main entry here. Back in the 1960s, the thirteenth generation of the aristocratic Yoda family converted its imposing Edo-period compound, conveniently located in a still-picturesque hamlet, into an inn. The original quarters, dating back 360 years and beautifully restored, are magnificent. Regrettably, they are devoted almost completely to common areas. Most of the guest rooms are in pedestrian concrete structures to the back. They're above average, to be sure, but pale in comparison to the modernizations of Seni, Aoni, and Kajika-an. The commodious, *hinoki* baths are pleasant enough but hardly traditional. There's no *rotenburo*. On the other hand, the gardens are bountiful, the bar-and-coffee shop in the ancient *miso* storage room is uniquely atmospheric and the food well above average. Try to book the lovely "Choja no ma," one of the only guest rooms in the old section.

Ōsawa Onsen Hotel

153-1 Osawa, Matsuzaki-cho, Shizuoka-ken

PHONE: 0558-43-0121   PRICE: C, D

TRANSPORTATION: From Shimoda Station on the Izu Kyuko Line, take the bus to Miyazaki for 45 minutes. Get off at Osawa Onsen Iriguchi and walk for 5 minutes.

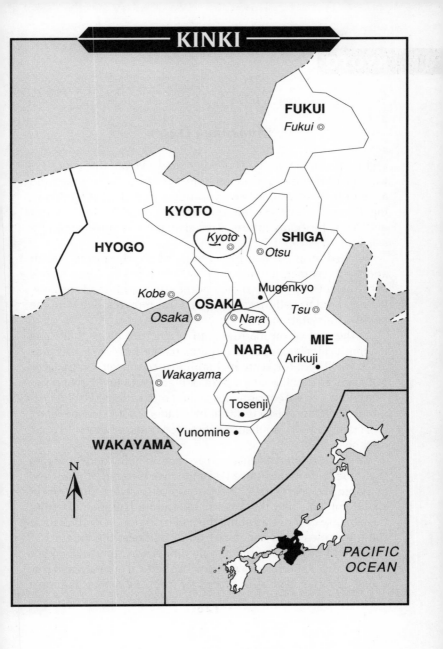

Mugenkyō Onsen

Right out of a picture book of early Showa Japan, this evocative wooden inn exudes pure Japan from its terra-cotta roof tiles and ancient lines to its dark-wood corridors and elegant landscaping. Except for a broken, antique cigarette machine in the lobby and TVs in the rooms, little else has changed here since Tsurunoya was built in 1929.

Perched atop a small promontory where the placid Nabari and Ika rivers merge, Tsurunoya is surrounded by dense woods at the end of a tiny road. There's nothing else man-made in sight. It's very hard to believe you're only a five-minute drive from the nearest train station.

At the end of the narrow road you'll spot an asphalt lane leading up for a couple of minutes to the inn's lush precinct. Soon you'll spot the separate bathhouse to the left, then a large water wheel dipping into a pool of black carp. Just beyond lies Tsurunoya's broad entryway, festooned with various tasteful bric-a-brac. The dark *genkan* is rather bare but a reading room just off it is crammed with all manner of stuffed birds, a baby wild boar, deer heads, etc.

We were escorted downstairs to a room called "Kaede" (maple) that, true to its name, looked over the river through a thick stand of maple and cherry trees. "Kaede" comprises two rooms, one of six tatami mats and the other of four-and-a-half mats. Despite the expanse of windows along the *roka* (corridor), it's rather dark. But it was pleasingly decorated, quiet, and near the toilet.

Served in the room, the simple dinner was, unusually, built around carp. *Koi-no-arai*, raw carp with a special mustard and *miso* sauce, is rather typical in places far from the ocean. But we'd never had carp *shabu-shabu*, which was the main dish. Many Japanese consider carp to be low class, but I rather enjoyed it. You dip the thin slices into a rich *miso* broth and let them cook for no more than thirty seconds.

Knowing that Mugenkyo was a *kosen*, I didn't necessarily expect much from the bath. But it surprised me. In an exotic design, the oval tub of smooth stones imbedded in concrete sits in the middle of a largish wooden room with warm lighting and considerable character. The clear, odorless water felt good.

Although in Kyoto Prefecture, getting here from the ancient capital isn't as easy as you might imagine. Mugenkyo is in a remote corner of the prefecture near the borders with Mie and Nara, there's no direct public-transportation link, and the road traffic in and out of Kyoto City is heavy. So it would be hard to combine a short sightseeing trip to Kyoto with a stay here. But it's relatively close to Nara. If you've got several days in the area, this place is well worth taking the time to enjoy.

Tsurunoya

Tayama, Minami Yamagi-mura, Kyoto-fu 619-14.

PHONE: 07439-3-0515   PRICE: D

TRANSPORTATION: From Kizu Station on the Katamachi and Nara lines, the train to Tsukigaseguchi on the Kansai Line takes about 30 minutes. Walk for 25 minutes or hop in a cab.

BY CAR: Drive 16.5 kilometers east of Kizu on Route 163, turn right at Tsukigaseguchi Station. Drive about 1.5 kilometers and turn right at the sign for Mugenkyo.

Arikuji Onsen

Known since the Kamakura Period (twelfth century) as a *reisen*, or spiritual spring with magical powers, Arikuji's silky water supposedly soothes not only the body but also the soul. It's said to be particularly good for drinking and the rice, tea and other water-based comestibles here are made with the spring water.

Testifying to the sacred tradition is the presence of both a temple and tiny shrine on the inn's shrouded grounds, as well as the observance of a fire-walking ceremony every November 12. But don't worry: no one will try to lay a religious trip on you. This is a very laid-back place run by a kind, unobtrusive elderly couple.

From the nearest bus stop you can walk or drive for 1.8 kilometers up a narrow, winding forest track lined with dense groves of ramrod cedars. Small Arikujiso lies secluded at the end, across from a pretty waterfall.

The inn has seen better days and isn't carefully managed. Metal sheeting covers most of the exterior walls, whose wood has fallen prey to the elements. The rooms are spare and tatty. Laundry hangs everywhere and the premises are strewn with provisions and junk. But none of this detracts much from the comely setting and authenticity of the place. While I wish it were better maintained, this quintessentially quaint hidden spring left me feeling most content.

Ask for the end room on the second floor of the building at the far side of the stream that runs right through the compound. This is the quietest, most private room in an already serene establishment. You can pay anywhere from 8,000 to 20,000 yen for the same room—the only variable being the dinner menu. The highest price gets you an *ise-ebi*, the closest thing to a real lobster that

Japanese waters yield. To me it's not worth the money. We opted for the 10,000-yen package and dined happily in the quaint, tatami-floored *shokudo*. Dinner included tuna and abalone *sashimi*, broiled *kamasu* (saury pike) and prawns, a *nabe* (stew) of the area's famed Matsuzaka beef, hot *chawan-nabe*, and the usual trimmings.

The concrete bathhouse doesn't look like much from the outside. But it houses two hospitable, dark-stone baths that conjure a cave-like feeling. The ever-so-slightly-cloudy water, coming out of the ground at a cool 24 degrees, is heated to perfection. Its high-alkaline content explains the silky softness. Signs in Japanese quaintly ask that you not use soap, as the introduction of such artificial elements might disturb the "spirit" of the water. That somehow doesn't preclude the presence of plastic stools and washbowls. The absence of a *rotenburo* in this bucolic setting seems a waste.

Arikuji's quietude assured me one of the best sleeps I've enjoyed at an *onsen*.

Arikujisō
Kii Nagashima-machi, Mie-ken 519-32
PHONE: 05974-7-2661   PRICE: B, C, D
TRANSPORTATION: From Kii Nagashima Station on the Kii Line, take the bus for Kawai for 10 minutes. Alight at Arikuji-guchi and walk for 25 minutes.
BY CAR: From Route 42 turn onto local road No. 11 at Kii Nagashima, drive about 3 kilometers and turn right at the inn's sign.

Tōsenji Onsen

Few visitors to Nara Prefecture stray beyond Yoshino, the hilly complex of temples and shrines famous for its cherry blossoms. But keep heading south toward Wakayama Prefecture and soon you'll be in remarkably rugged, unpopulated territory. It's some of the wildest country I've seen in Japan and an amazing contrast to the plain on which the cities of Nara and Uji reside.

There aren't many *onsen* to pick from in these parts but this place is well worth seeking out. Tosenji lies above a wide river bed on a little-trafficked road off the main highway. At the far end of the enclave, lonely Yadoyu no Sato clings to the river bank, smack-dab against the road. This and the small inn's utilitarian appearance put me off at first. But once we reached our room there was little doubt we'd found a winner. Called "Taro," the room was actually a corner suite comprising a six-tatami-mat sleeping area, an eight-mat living room, Western toilet, and long *roka* (corridor) between the tatami and wall-to-wall windows on the north and west sides of the quarters. This provided plenty of light and a panoramic view over the river. Ornate shoji, rich wood ceilings, a large *kotatsu*, and immaculate furnishings combined to make this one of the most pleasant and memorable rooms we've encountered.

Family-run and hospitable, unassuming Yadoyu no Sato is lovingly maintained throughout. Potted flowers grace the corridors. At the small *genkan* you'll spot several photos of Prince Ayanomiya and Princess Kiko visiting the inn with friends while they were in college. Despite the roadside location, we found it remarkably quiet and comfortable

Our beautifully presented dinner lived up to the surroundings. Prepared by the inn's master, it included a hearty wild-boar *nabe*, raw slices of venison arranged in the shape of flowers, broiled eel, grilled *ayu*, and delicious dabs of mountain vegetables. This was served in a private room upstairs from our quarters.

The baths here are uninspired but inviting. I found the indoor water too hot but the small adjoining *rotenburo* felt great. Some of my longest soaks ever were here, augmented by stunning views over the river. Although the *rotenburo* are sexually segregated, the men's side can be easily "integrated" at night.

For 15,000 yen per person and no service charge, Yadoyu no Sato is a true bargain. We left reluctantly and gratified.

Yadoyu no Sato
Tosenji, Totsukawa-mura, Yoshino-gun, Nara-ken 637-13
PHONE: 07466-3-0020   PRICE: C
TRANSPORTATION: From Gojo Station on the Wakayama Line, take the bus bound for Shingu, Yunomine Onsen, or Totsukawa for 2 hours, 30 minutes. Get off at Totsukawa Mura Yakuba-mae and phone the inn to pick you up there.
BY CAR: Drive 72 kilometers south of Gojo on Route 370, then travel south on Route 168 for 72 kilometers.

Yunomine Onsen

Along with the likes of Dai and Doroyu *onsen*, this is one of the few hot-spring villages I enjoy. Like the others, it's in an isolated, natural setting, quaint, lacking high-rises and shopping districts, and serviced by a tiny street with little traffic.

Compact Yunomine contains two inns, several large *minshuku*, two shops, and a *sunakku*. This spring claims to be Japan's oldest, although several others make the same assertion. Regardless, Yunomine boasts a terrific legend.

According to the story, in the early 1400s an aristocrat poisoned in an assassination attempt by the Ashikaga shogunate fled with his lover from today's Fujisawa in Kanagawa Prefecture to this mountain redoubt to successfully nurse himself back to health. Today you can bathe in the same tiny, stone tub he allegedly used. It's called "Tsubo no Yu" and is in the middle of the village, between the road and the stream. For 230 yen it's well worth a dip. Just below this sheltered *rotenburo* local folk flock to fill large plastic containers with spring water for drinking and to boil eggs.

Azumaya dates back more than 400 years. Little from then remains; today's inn is a hodgepodge of buildings linked by interior corridors. The complex is modestly attractive though unextraordinary. But the welcome is unusually cordial and the women staff are all clad in tasteful kimono. Be sure to reserve a room in the oldest part of the inn, at the top of the slope. These are more atmospheric than the one we had and are shielded from the occasional vehicle noise. They don't feature private toilets, however.

Azumaya's food is unremarkable but perfectly acceptable. The rice, breakfast gruel, and coffee on offer in the souvenir corner are all prepared with *onsen* water. This seemed to make them richer-tasting than usual.

The highlight here is the baths. Indoors, they're spacious and resplendently clad in dark wood, including the tubs, which contain clear, perfect-temperature water with a subtle but noticeable mineral odor. The adjoining rocky *rotenburo* are small but pleasant. Look hard enough and you'll find two unmarked *kazokuburo* (family baths) down a short, tiny corridor to the left just before the entrances to the main baths. Although the inn was fairly full on our Friday-night visit in early December, the baths were remarkably unpopulated.

If you're in a party mood, try the intimate karaoke bar across from the souvenir area. It's well insulated from the guest quarters and frequented by locals. The mama-san was relatively chatty but kept serving me brandy when I ordered whisky.

Azumaya
Yunomine, Hongu-machi, Wakayama-ken
PHONE: 07354-2-0012   PRICE: D
TRANSPORTATION: From Shingu Station on the Kisei Line, a bus takes about 75 minutes.
BY CAR: From Route 42 at Shingu, head northwest on Route 168, turn left on Route 311 and it's about 10 kilometers more.

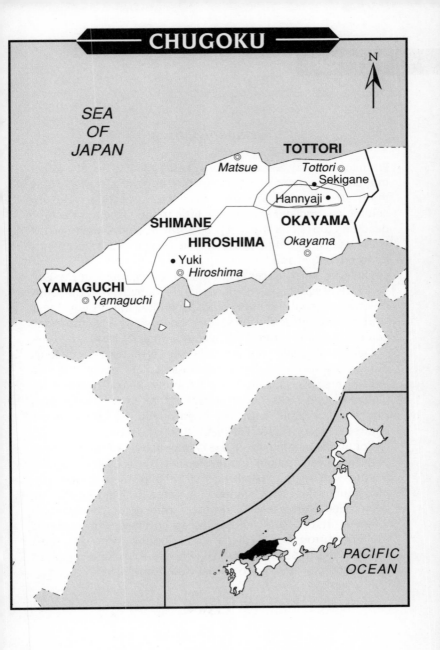

Sekigane Onsen

From the highway, Sekigane looks like it's going to be yet another mundane *onsen* town. But once you turn into the narrow and dark main street, you'll discover otherwise. It's relatively un-commercialized and quaint, with little traffic. Onseiro sits at the dead-end top of this street. If you're driving, pass Onseiro on the left and bear left onto a dirt road. The inn's parking lot is about a hundred meters away.

Onseiro, which traces its origins to a tea-house in the Edo period, looks pretty pedestrian from the outside. And the lobby is nothing special. But once you've penetrated the interior, things start looking better. The inn's two wooden wings face onto a lush garden area built around the mixed-bathing *rotenburo*.

Our room, "Tsuki," was one of the best. Near the end of a long, dim, wooden corridor, it was eight tatami mats and oblong with a sitting area overlooking the garden and *rotenburo*. The toilet was Japanese-style. "Tsuki" is conveniently situated near the fetching *kazokuburo*, or family bath. The tiny wooden tub for two is im-planted in a stone floor. Flowers festoon the room.

For public bathing, avoid the cramped and utilitarian indoor baths and head straight for the *rotenburo*. This is Onseiro's nicest feature, well worth maximizing your time in. The two *hinoki* (cy-press) tubs offer comfy, shimmering water so clear that it's long been called "*Shirogane no Yu*" (water of white gold). The different-temperature tubs are sheltered by an attractive wood-raftered roof and surrounded by pretty stone flooring. More than most *rotenburo*, this one is not for the shy. There are no changing rooms and the pool is exposed to partial view from the inn.

Visiting the *rotenburo* at night, we encountered a threesome of local senior citizens very much into their cups. The sight of two big foreigners enlivened their partying mood and we spent the next hour being plied with all manner of drink. Indeed, the young manager who had shown us to our room had said he was "refreshed" to see our faces since so few non-Japanese visit Sekigane.

Dinner proved rather ho-hum, with the major exception of bountiful crab legs and a nice crab *nabe* (stew). We weren't expecting this in the far mountain reaches of Tottori. Our elderly maid, when asked, said we could have dinner "anytime." So we suggested 6:30. "How about a little before six?" she responded. Oh, well.

Sekigane Onsen celebrates festivals on the third Saturday of April and on October 7. Guests on those days can drink as much beer and saké as they like for a nominal fee.

Onseirō
1230 Sekigane-juku, Sekigane-machi, Tohaku-gun, Tottori-ken 682-04
PHONE: 0858-45-3311   PRICE: D
TRANSPORTATION: From Kurayoshi Station on the San-in Line, the bus to Sekigane Onsen takes 35 minutes. Then walk for 15 minutes.
BY CAR: From Hiruzen I. C. on the Yonago Expressway, drive 7 kilometers on Route 482 to Route 313. Turn left and drive 12 kilometers more.

Hannyaji Onsen

This captivating, unusual *onsen* for some reason doesn't show up on most maps. Maybe because it's so close to the large *onsen* town of Okutsu. At any rate, it's worth seeking out for its lovely *hanare* and grounds. In many ways, it's the picture of the perfect hidden hot spring.

From busy Route 179 leading up to Okutsu, you have to walk down a long, zigzagging stone stairway into the ravine where Hannyaji resides. Before long you'll catch sight of the owner's large, sumptuously thatched home. Just beyond lies the tiny temple to which Hannyaji owes its name and then the bathhouse. To the right, across a stream, rest two demure, unpainted wooden buildings that house the inn's three rooms. These classic structures grace a park-like riverside clearing studded with boulders, small waterfalls, and shapely pines. It is indeed a lovely setting.

Our room, "Matsu," was a traditionally designed cottage unto itself. Its eight-tatami-mat room was unassuming but elegant, providing a delightful corner view over the stream and boulders. Sporting a large *kotatsu*, these were very comfy, exclusive quarters. The toilet, however, was Japanese-style.

For such an evocative setting, Hannyaji's shed-like bathhouse is incongruously concrete. The owners could have done a much better job. But it's tucked into a corner of the compound so isn't much of an eyesore. And once you're in the mixed bath, you should be satisfied. Dim and somewhat cavelike, it feels properly primitive and even intimate. The water is tepid, so much so that we barely got warm on our December visit. It should be good for lingering dips during summer.

The food here is mostly standard fare—cold tempura; warm, grilled rockfish; *chawanmushi*; and steamed vegetables. Highlights included a scrumptious *tororo* flecked with *yuzu*, raw trout, and *mazegohan*. This was served to us in the *hanare* by the owner's kind, talkative wife.

Hannyaji's only real drawback is its proximity to the highway just above. You can't see the traffic but you can certainly hear it. I'm especially sensitive to noise, though. My companion didn't seem bothered at all.

Hannyaji Onsen
Okutsu Kawanishi, Okutsu-machi, Tomata-gun, Okayama-ken
PHONE: 0868-52-0602   PRICE: D
TRANSPORTATION: From Tsuyama Station on the Tsuyama Line, take the bus bound for Okutsu for 70 minutes. Get off at Otsuri Onsen Mae and walk for 10 minutes.
BY CAR: From Innoshou I. C. on the Chugoku Jidoshado, take Route 179 north for about 26 kilometers.

Yuki Onsen

Although the photos I'd seen of this *onsen* weren't very inspiring, a visit proved Yuki a beguiling find. I wouldn't go terribly out of my way to get here, but if you're in the area, especially in late March, check it out. In a hushed ravine, most of Yuki's half-dozen inns crouch before a fetching stream that separates them from a quiet thoroughfare lined with magnificent cherry trees. By far the most attractive inn is wooden Midoriso. Ask for the first-floor corner room facing the stream. Until recently, nearby Yunoyama Onsen was one of Japan's most adorable hot-spring hamlets. But in 1993 it was irreparably and unforgivably scarred by an unconscionable concrete European-style spa of massive proportions dreamed up by the mayor as a way to boost tourism. This is one tourist who will never go near Yunoyama again, much to my profound regret.

Midorisō
2661 Tada, Yuki-cho, Saiki-gun, Hiroshima-ken
PHONE: 0829-85-0321   PRICE: C, D
TRANSPORTATION: From Itsukaichi Station on the Sanyo Line, the bus for Yuki Onsen takes 1 hour. Then walk for about 5 minutes.

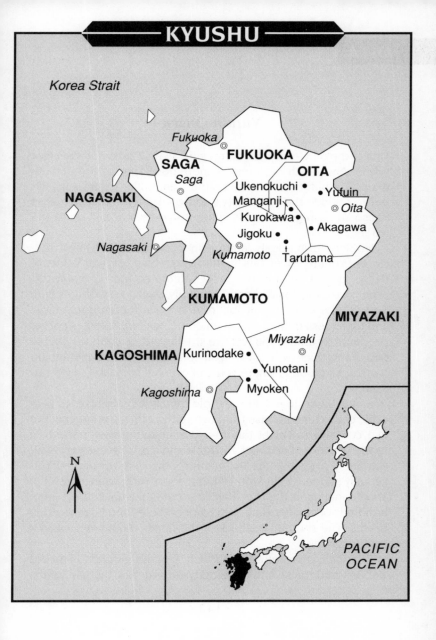

Yufuin Onsen

This is the only exception to my rule against inns in large *onsen* towns. And much of Yufuin is more developed and mundane than its reputation for beauty and tranquillity would suggest. But to exclude the supremely traditional, salubriously situated Sanso Yamashige from this guide would be a disservice to the reader.

Hidden down a leafy lane in what's probably the finest precinct of Yufuin proper, this hushed, tiny refuge lies near Kamenoi Besso, one of Yufuin's two most celebrated inns and way too expensive for inclusion here. Thankfully, Sanso Yamashige offers up a similar superb atmosphere in a much more intimate way and for far less money. Although dinner isn't included as part of the package, unless you feel like striking out on your own, Mr. or Mrs. Yamashige will escort you to the elegant restaurant on Kamenoi's grounds where you can eat well for just a few thousand yen.

Sanso Yamashige's 300 year-old thatched building of impeccable character comprises just two suites. Mine, the larger of the two, contained an eight-tatami-mat main room, a six-mat sitting room, Western-style toilet and sink, and a private entrance—all extremely pleasing. The two main rooms were divided by gorgeously grained, light-wood sliding doors with a narrow strip of shoji paneling at the top. Making up the unusual ceilings were hundreds of slender, darkened bamboo poles and huge wooden beams. The shoji at the back of the larger room overlooked a simple garden.

Sharing Sanso Yamashige's lush, languid grounds is an old wooden bathhouse and the elderly Yamashiges' tasteful home.

The simple stone bath is dimly lit, moderately warm, and able to accommodate only a couple of bathers at a time. Most romantic. (Mrs. Yamashige brags that unlike many larger establishments in Yufuin, she doesn't mix her *o-yu* with regular water). Walking to and from the bath at night, the ethereal lighting, absolute still-ness, and vintage coziness of the compound made me wonder if I was a time traveler.

Unfortunately, Mr. Yamashige was laid up with the flu during my visit. He's apparently quite the friendly fellow. But he'd be hard-pressed to match his colorful wife's gift of gab. During our several extended encounters she regaled me with stories about the antiques bedecking my quarters, Kamenoi Besso's friendly designs on Sanso Yamashige, her family's connections to the rich and famous, and the occasional memorable foreigners who have passed through. She speaks a smattering of English and cooks up a mean breakfast served, during my December visit, at the civilized hour of 9 A.M. and next to the stove in a snug alcove beside the kitchen.

A couple of tips: Ask for the larger suite, the one nearer the bath. And see if Mrs. Yamashige will remove the chiming clock, which incongruously and incessantly intrudes.

Sansō Yamashige
Dakemoto, Yufuin-machi, Oita-gun, Oita-ken 879-51
PHONE: 0977-84-3166   PRICE: C
TRANSPORTATION: From Yufuin Station, a taxi takes about 8 minutes.
          BY CAR: If driving, make your way to the station and ask the tourist office for directions.

✳ ✳ ✳

Ukenokuchi Onsen

After spending several days exploring the *onsen* adorning this quarter of Kyushu, I concluded that Onoya is one of the only places worth recommending. That's not so much a reflection on this worthy inn as it is on the pitiful commercialization, lack of taste, and unfortunate settings of its somewhat distant neighbors.

The hamlet of Ukenokuchi embraces two inns, a relatively nice public bath, a colorful traditional store, and several dwellings. It's down a steep incline from a quiet highway that courses through one of Kyushu's most scenic and undeveloped mountain districts. It's not the comeliest of settings and small Onoya unfortunately faces its larger, ugly competitor.

But to enter Onoya's spare, dim *genkan* is to step into the world of 1920s *shibui*. This word, along with *wabi* and *sabi*, is one of the most common in describing the understated elegance and subtlety of traditional Japan. Dictionaries tend to render *shibui* as "refined," "sober," "astringent," or "tasteful." The Nobel Prize-winning novelist Yasunari Kawabata, not even a Kyushu-ite, appreciated Onoya so much on his first visit that he went back.

If at all possible, reserve the corner suite where Kawabata stayed. By far the best in the house, it comprises six- and eight-tatami-mat rooms, wooden *roka* corridors on two sides, and expansive windows. As the only upstairs lodging, it's private and quiet. The *okami-san* (landlady of the inn) told me it hasn't been changed since Kawabata slept there in 1953. I managed to get it for just 15,000 yen as a single. The only downside was the long trip to the lavatory.

The main corridor running from the stairway at the bottom of my room and the *genkan* to the lavatory, bath, and dining rooms bisects the inn's other half-dozen rooms. The corridor is wooden, dark, and *shibui*. Speaking of the baths, they're simplicity defined. In snug, wood-clad rooms the tiny, cement tubs can handle only two bathers at a time. Hottish but quickly adjustable with a jolt of cold water, they contain slightly murky water redolent with minerals.

For dinner I enjoyed my own private dining room adjacent to the kitchen. The landlady's charming daughter popped in from time to time to explain the various exotic courses, which ranged from grated mountain potatoes laced with an obscure herb to field snails in escargot-like shells, whole fresh-water crab, river "seaweed," a mountain-stream fish called *enoha* (a kind of trout) that I'd never before encountered, a delicious corn concoction steamed in leaves, *norimaki sushi* made from *soba* instead of rice, mushroom *takikomigohan*, tempura of wild fungi, gingko nuts, the berries of wild-potato plants, and more.

Just as Kawabata once did, I'm also plotting my return.

Onoya
Iida Kogen, Kokonoe-machi, Kusu-gun, Oita-ken 879-49
PHONE: 09737-9-2413 PRICE: C
TRANSPORTATION: From Bungo Nakamura Station on the Kyudai Line, take the bus bound for Sujiyu or Iida Kogen for 25 minutes. Get off at Ukenokuchi and walk for 5 minutes.
BY CAR: From Route 210 just west of Bungo Nakamura station, head south on local road No. 40. Turn left at the sign posted for Sujiyu and drive about 10 kilometers.

Akagawa Onsen

The picture of a 1950s mountain lodge, quaint and lonely Akagawaso clearly belongs to another era. Hurrah! Akagawa's spring and its condensed particulates—*yunohana*—long enjoyed a reputation for their effectiveness against venereal disease. Until the late 1950s, a sulfur factory worked the site. But then the owners closed down that business and put up today's simple clapboard structure. It contains about ten small, basic, well-kept rooms upstairs, a utilitarian dining room on the main floor, and compact, sexually segregated rock baths. These feature deeply blue-gray water heated up just right from its natural twenty-six degrees. There's also a mixed-bathing *rotenburo* sitting beneath a lovely waterfall but the water isn't heated. We weren't about to try it on our cold December visit but it's probably pleasant in summer. These days the water gets special note for its effectiveness against athlete's foot, among other ailments. Also, bear in mind that Route 442, above which Akagawaso resides, is one of Kyushu's most scenic.

Akagawasō
4008 Kuju, Kuju-machi, Oita-ken 878-02
PHONE: 0974-76-0081   PRICE: A
TRANSPORTATION: From Bungo Takeda Station on the Hohi Line, take the bus bound for Kurokawa Onsen for 45 minutes to Kuju Kogenso. Walk for 30 minutes.

Manganji Onsen

Quaint Manganji is a village that time has passed by. Very little can have changed since the 1960s with one exception: Zuiunso. In 1993 it was expanded from a *minshuku* into a small inn with rare good taste and imagination. It doesn't detract at all from the traditional charm of the village.

Several new, tan, half-timbered buildings now grace the hill above Zuiunso's original sixty-five-year old structure. Two of these structures, at the top of the hill, are *hanare*, or private cottages, and it's in one of these that you should stay. For no more than you'd pay for a room in the sterile main building you get a six-tatami-mat entryway-sitting area and an eight-mat main room, both adorned with ornate woodwork and unusual sliding doors that combine shoji and *fusuma*. There's also a sink and Western toilet. Both of these utterly silent dwellings are surrounded by pretty wooden fences and they command a fine view over the inn's compound and the village.

Within a few steps you can reach the pristine wooden bath-house just below. The indoor walls are of *hinoki*, as is the lip of the good-sized flagstone tub. The high ceilings and moderate water temperature enhance the bathing pleasure. Manganji's spring water is artificially heated, clear and odorless. Outside lies a cozy *rotenburo* with lukewarm water—perfect for long dips.

When dinner time arrives, make your way back down the wood-roofed walkways to the original structure, where you will have checked in. At night, the lanes are lovingly lit with lamps under baskets. You're now about to feast on one of the most dazzling meals available at any *onsen* inn for the price.

We were ushered to a rustic, yet refined, four-and-a-half-mat room in the deep reaches of the atmospheric, farmhouse-like building. The table was an enormous slab of a tree, the rafters darkened bamboo, and the lighting non-fluorescent.

Then began a steady flow of unforgettable courses, exquisitely prepared and served fresh and warm. The appetizers included a three-colored okra pâté served with with mustard sauce; raw carp with onions in an innovative sauce; marinated chicken with spinach; and steamed turnips with mushrooms. Then came steamed trout stuffed with egg, vegetables, and *miso* sauce; a rich soup of duck and spinach stuffed with ground trout; a steamed turnip stuffed with ground fowl and covered in *miso* sauce; baked mountain potatoes laced with finely sliced burdock; a superb carp *misoshiru*; and rice flecked with *takuwan* pickles.

This was one of the finest, most inventive meals I've encountered at an *onsen*. And one of the very few where courses were served one at a time as soon as they were prepared. All in all, this is a warmly welcoming, conscientious inn of incredible value.

Zuiunsō
Manganji, Minami Oguni-machi, Aso-gun, Kumamoto-ken 869-24
PHONE: 0967-42-0825   PRICE: B
TRANSPORTATION: From Aso Station on the Hohi Line, take the bus found for Tsuetate for 40 minutes. Change at Ichihara to the Manganji-bound bus, which takes about 10 minutes.
BY CAR: 2 kilometers south of Oguni on Route 212, turn east onto local road No. 40 for about 6 kilometers.

✳ ✳ ✳

Kurokawa Onsen

This neoclassical inn reminded me of Daikokuya at Itamuro Onsen for its interesting marriage of the old and new. Built strictly along enduring Japanese lines, the two-story, isolated Yamamizuki graces a rolling highland plain one kilometer above compact but densely developed Kurokawa Onsen. Its exterior walls are pleasingly beige and half-timbered, the multi-leveled roof clad in dark terra-cotta tiles. A beautiful sight to behold.

Breach its portals and you encounter a creative version of East-meets-West. The spare, blond-wood *genkan* is uncompromisingly Japanese. Step up to the lobby and you'll find minimalist, contemporary Western decor with tasteful pink carpeting. Unobtrusive classical music fills in the background.

A kimono-clad *obasan* showed us to our first-floor room, the best in the house, named "Shurei." Spread out over a capacious twelve-and-a-half tatami mats, it was simple, pristine, and elegant. The plaster walls were an earthy brownish-green, the ceilings of light wood. Most striking were the unusual, half-moon *yukimi* shoji overlooking a large but unpretentious garden. Our accommodations also included a private, wooden bath and Western toilet.

Don't waste time checking out the public indoor baths except for a proper shower and shampoo. They're incongruously done up in pink tile. Head straight for the main *rotenburo*, one of the best in this book. It's spacious, well-situated next to a timbered stream and waterfall, and lovingly laid out. A wooden pavilion in the middle of the pool shelters three *utaseyu*—hot, pelting streams of water pouring out of bamboo spouts about three meters overhead. These make for a great shoulder and neck massage. The changing room is of classic, wooden design. Most important, the clear, odorless water is just the right temperature. There's a smaller women's *rotenburo* next to a tiny thatched structure above the main *rotenburo* but the latter was sexually integrated on our visit. At night, outdoor walkways in the *rotenburo* environs are evocatively lit by flaming gas lanterns.

Yamamizuki's food is somewhat innovative and generally above average. Our appetizer included cold sliced duck and room-temperature tempura with prawns and *sayori*. This was followed by *nasu dengaku*, or broiled eggplant smeared with a sweet *miso* sauce; an excellent *sashimi* of red snapper, squid and tuna; piping-hot, broiled *yamame* river fish; steamed spinach, gingko nuts and bream; an indifferent beef fillet; and a nice mushroom *nabe*.

Lovely in most respects, Yamamizuki sins in a few. The coin lockers on the way to the bath are an insulting eyesore, as are the adjacent vending machines. The management is a bit too quick to whip out vacuum cleaners in the morning. Doors to the outside were inexplicably kept open in the midst of winter. Overall, though, this is a charming place and far more serene than Kurokawa Onsen proper.

> **Yamamizuki**
> Oku Kurokawa Onsen, Oguni-machi, Aso-gun, Kumamoto-ken 869-24
> PHONE: 0967-44-0336   PRICE: C, D
> TRANSPORTATION: From Bungo Taketa Station on the Hohi Line, take the bus to Kurokawa Onsen for 55 minutes. The inn will pick you up there.
> BY CAR: Enter Kurokawa just off Route 442 between Oguni and Taketa, and turn right after about 200 meters. Drive 2 kilometers more.

✳ ✳ ✳

Tarutama Onsen

I was a bit disappointed when first catching sight of this rambling, humdrum-looking but popular mountain inn that I'd barely been able to reserve months in advance for a Friday in December. As the exterior suggested, the quarters turned out to be a bit institutional and worn, and the meals were rather ordinary. Plenty of over-compensating delights awaited, however.

Take the service. When I phoned a few days ahead to report that I'd become a party of one, instead of two as reserved, the manager sounded crestfallen. Though completely unaware I was doing a guide, he'd assigned me one of the best rooms in the house. Single occupancy was not in his economic interests. But he quickly complied and upon my arrival treated me famously. I got the room originally reserved—"Sakura" in the *bekkan*, or annex. Though nothing special, it offered a nice view. My engaging, kimono-clad maid told me "Sakura" was one of her favorites.

That doesn't necessarily mean the most expensive. For a modestly higher price you can get a room on the first floor of the *bekkan* with a private bath. But the tubs are so tiny and charmless as to be worthless given the superb public baths at hand.

Indeed, I rank single-inn Tarutama's collection of baths as best in the land. Tops is the mixed-bathing *rotenburo*, above the road fronting Yamaguchi Ryokan. These beautiful, rocky half-roofed pools stretch beneath two magnificent waterfalls whose illumination at night is celestial. The clear, odorless water felt perfect on a chill December night and despite a jam-packed inn, I was essentially uninterrupted on my visit. This is unsurpassed outdoor bathing.

Coming a very close second at Yamaguchi Ryokan is "Kajikanoyu," the splendidly thatched *han-rotenburo* within the inn's grounds. "Kajikanoyu" boasts two sets of pools, between which men and women alternate. On my visit, by far the best side went to men in the evening and women in the morning. Dazzlingly beamed and stone-lantern lit, this houses a tastefully wrought Jacuzzi-style tub and a pleasurable herb bath in which a muslin bag full of local flora has been immersed. On the other side, the main bath is essentially indoors, opening onto two outdoor *goemonburo* tubs. Vat-shaped and accommodating just one bather at a time, they're named after a legendary figure who was boiled alive in such a pot. The water in all of Kajikanoyu's baths is a slightly murky grayish-green and most excellent.

Yamaguchi Ryokan's large but understated main indoor bath (the men's, at least) boasts a vaulted, beamed ceiling and wood-lined changing room. The *hinoki*-edged, tile-lined, triangular tub looks through massive glass sliding doors over part of the compound. Ignore Yamaguchi's *kazokuburo*, or private family bath. It's intolerably hot and boring.

Yamaguchi Ryokan
2331 Kawayo, Choyo-son, Aso-gun, Kumamoto-ken 869-14
PHONE: 09676-7-0006   PRICE: B, C
TRANSPORTATION: From Aso Shimoda Station on the Minami-Aso
Line, the bus to Tarutama Onsen takes 20 minutes.
BY CAR: Or from Route 325 south of Mount Aso, turn north
at Choyo-mura and follow the signs for about 6
kilometers.

✳ ✳ ✳

Jigoku Onsen

Just several hundred meters above Tarutama's Yamaguchi Ryokan,
Seifuso offers a different spring and a considerably different
ethic. Against the eye-popping, visually sensual, and fine-water
baths of Tarutama, better-known Jigoku's are primitive, down-
home, murky-water affairs for a more purist bathing crowd. Jigoku
also boasts far more interesting dining. Try to stay at both inns if
you can since they offer such contrastingly wonderful aspects of
the hidden-spring experience in very close proximity. If you only
have time for one, stay at the less comfortable but more authentic Seifuso and visit Yamaguchi's waterfall *rotenburo* after dinner.

At Seifuso we got much more indifferent service than at
Yamaguchi Ryokan. The initial reception was matter-of-fact and
our maid dour. Our room, one of the cheapest in the house,
overlooked the parking lot and was a plain six-and-a-half tatami
mats plus a sitting area and Japanese-style toilet. You can do
better by paying more.

But one comes here less for niceties than for the eating and
bathing. Once you've arrived at your room, the maid will present
you with menus complete with pictures of the various dinner
courses on offer. You can choose from about five alternatives
including several kinds of *nabe, teppan-yaki*, and *kushi-yaki*. We
opted for the "Jigoku" course, which cost an extra 1,000 yen per

person and included duck, venison-and-vegetable *teppan-yaki*, and *inoshishi nabe*.

Meals are served in an ancient, barn-like structure up the hill in back of the inn. Converted into a marvelously rustic dining room in the late 1980s, it's rivaled only by Seni's dining area for sensual delight. Softly lit, half-timbered, and richly beamed, it contains about twenty large, log-slabbed booths each built around its own *irori* (sunken hearth). You sit around the fire *horigotatsu*-style, with your legs dangling below the *irori*. Dozens of pheasant carcasses hang from the walls, a huge wooden vat dangles from the ceiling, and *tansu* chests dot the wood-planked corridors. With plenty of help from the traditionally garbed staff you cook your own meal. Ours was enormous and tasty.

Breakfast, served in the same delightful place, is built around a *sansai* buffet. Bread, butter, and coffee are available self-service style. A loop-like trough of water circulates baskets of seaweed, *natto* (fermented soybeans), and raw eggs among the booths. You can fry the eggs on a griddle at your table if you want.

Seifuso's spare, large indoor baths feature aged *hinoki* throughout and murky, sulfurous water. But you're much better off heading for the separate, more relaxed bath complex called "Suzumenoyu." It comprises segregated, small, wooden indoor baths and several chockablock *han-rotenburo* tubs that are mixed-bathing. The water temperature varies from tub to tub. Some are lukewarm enough to allow hours of uninterrupted immersion. Here bathers banter with each other and women smear mud on their faces. A most colorful scene.

Seifūsō

2327 Kawayo, Choyo-son, Aso-gun, Kumamoto-ken 869-14
PHONE: 09676-7-0005   PRICE: B, C
TRANSPORTATION: From Aso Shimoda Station on the Minami-Aso Line, take the bus bound for Tarutama Onsen for 30 minutes. Get off at Kokumin shukusha-mae and walk for 5 minutes.

BY CAR: From Route 325 south of Mount Aso, turn north at Choyo-mura and follow the signs for about 6 kilometers.

Kurokawa Onsen

Sanga Ryokan is a comely, single-inn compound of classical buildings in a verdant ravine a couple of kilometers below Kurokawa Onsen proper. Entering the dimly lit, impressively beamed *genkan*, you'd think you were encountering antiquity. But this main building was completed in 1993, and most of the precinct's renovation is almost as new. They've done a superb job preserving antiquarian values. The baths range from rustic wooden and stone indoor versions to separate outdoor pavilions containing huge, sunken, vat-like tubs that can hold several bathers at a time. There's also a salubrious *rotenburo*. This is a worthy, less expensive alternative to tonier Yamamizuki up the road (p. 148).

Sanga Ryokan
Kurokawa Onsen, Minami Oguni-machi, Aso-gun, Kumamoto-ken 869
PHONE: 0967-44-0906   PRICE: B, C
TRANSPORTATION: See directions to Yamamizuki at Kurokawa Onsen (p. 150).

Yunotani Onsen

Along with Gajoen at Myoken Onsen (p. 156) this is one of the only two inns in the concrete menagerie of northeastern Kagoshima-ken that I would patronize. Better than that, I highly recommended it. Although Gajoen is far more sensual and romantic, the more isolated, down-home Yunotani Sanso comes closer to the true hidden hot-spring experience. It's a place for serious bathers and also a remarkable bargain.

After a couple of hours' driving through one horrific *onsen* town after another, my Swiss companion and I were despairing of finding a decent inn for the night. But our noses finally led us in the right direction down a leafy mountain road and before long we caught sight of Yunotani Sanso's sign. Turning left up a narrow track we were at the *genkan* within five minutes. The isolated inn feels lost in nature, surrounded by dense forest and far enough from the main road to be absolutely quiet. Maybe not very traditional to look at from the outside, having been rebuilt in 1992, the two-story structure still fits with its arboreal surroundings better than most such places.

We were warmly welcomed by the informal *okami-san*, who immediately escorted us to our bright, simple, and immaculate eight-tatami-mat room. The shoji paneling featured a subtle leaf pattern. We had our own toilet. However, without much atmosphere to soak up in the room, we headed quickly for the baths.

They turned out to be first-class. The relatively spacious, all-wood indoor one felt wonderfully antique; it obviously hadn't been redone in 1992. The main tub was relatively small, though, and in mid-afternoon on a Tuesday in December it was crowded.

My friend and I pressed ahead, however, and squeezed in. The water was pretty hot, cloudy and infused with fine sulfur *yunohana*. Our fellow bathers didn't take long to venture conversation, which we happily joined. But before long we couldn't resist the urge to try the *rotenburo*. It turned out to be empty, alluring, secluded, and snug. We indulged in many a dip here, always alone. You must watch your timing, though. Bathing hours for men and women alternate every two hours.

If the baths were heavenly, the food was even better. Served in a pretty six-mat private room, dinner was sensational. We feasted on superb *sashimi* of snapper, abalone, yellowtail, *sayori*, and *uni*; a hot rock-grilled duck, eggplant, corn, peppers, and richly marbled horsemeat; succulent, warm, stuffed eggplant; a wild-boar *nabe*; chicken, fish and vegetables in a rich *miso* broth; warm, homemade noodles; a large clam grilled with salt; jellyfish in sesame sauce; and more. We got all this by opting for the highest price, which still kept us within my "B" category.

Yunotani Sanso is clearly a winner.

> **Yunotani Sansō**
> 4970 Takachidaka, Makizono-cho, Kagoshima-ken
> PHONE: 0995-78-2852 PRICE: B, C
> TRANSPORTATION: From Kirishima Station on the Nippo Line, take the bus bound for Hayashida Onsen for 30 minutes. Get off at Yunotani Onsen Iriguchi and walk for 15 minutes.
> BY CAR: From Route 233 between Maruo Onsen and Kirishima shrine, turn north at the sign and drive about 1 kilometer.

* * *

Myōken Onsen

Once among the most pastoral of *onsen* settings, northeastern Kagoshima Prefecture has been seriously disfigured by the virulent overdevelopment of its two-dozen or so springs. Among the many *onsen* establishments in the area, Gajoen is a gem in a rockpile.

You'd never imagine so upon catching sight of the generally blighted Myoken Onsen, whose depressing concrete inns morosely line a ravine on Highway 223. In fact, you have to look pretty hard to find the obscure sign pointing up to Gajoen. It's worth the effort. For here, shrouded in a grove on the far bank of the river running parallel to Route 223, hides one of Kyushu's *onsen* treasures.

Arranged like a tiny hamlet, hushed Gajoen contains about a dozen thatched and terra-cotta-roofed structures. All are sublimely traditional. Your room will be in one of these cottages, though the only ones within my 20,000-yen limit were the tile-roofed ones. Along the compound's path, colorful chickens and roosters strut and peck at the ground. A small pavilion contains a working *irori* (sunken hearth) surrounded by seats. There's not a vending machine to be found.

Our room, "Mizu," was part of a duplex set back a bit from the lane. Stepping up from the stone *genkan*, we felt we'd entered our own little house. The eight-tatami-mat main room was tastefully understated, with a wooden ceiling and half-timbered, light-brown plaster walls. On the far side, a stark, dark-planked sink area faced the river just below. Off to the right was a similar, larger area with toilet and a refrigerator. Unfortunately, there were no chairs from which to enjoy the lovely view over the river.

Dinner was served in the room by a maid in country-style garb. The meal proved simple—a delicate tempura of assorted leaves; excellent broiled *ayu*; a rich, white *miso* soup brimming with vegetables; superbly rendered *yaki-onigiri* (grilled rice balls); and other goodies. A bit modest for the price, I thought, but well executed. Our gorgeous chopstick wrappers, for example, had our names beautifully inscribed in brush strokes. Breakfast helped compensate for the small dinner. Served in a large thatched dining pavilion right out of an ancient farm, the meal included warm, fresh-squeezed milk, homemade rolls, huge eggs, and the normal trimmings.

We visited Gajoen not long after a major typhoon devastated Kyushu. One of the victims was Gajoen's *rotenburo*, so it wasn't back up and running yet. But perched next to the river it looked promising. The main baths sit in a refined, log-beamed pavilion that's partially open-air but too enclosed to be a *rotenburo*. The small concrete and rock tubs feel primitive and offer up murky, sulfur- and iron-infused water. The illumination at night is evocative. After our post-dinner dip we emerged to find a small tub of free-for-the-taking iced beer and oolong tea sitting on the path. But we passed that up to accept the invitation to drink free, warm *shochu* in the snug *irori* pavilion with most of Gajoen's other guests. The liquor supply seemed endless and a wonderful time was had by all.

> **Gajoen**
> Myoken Onsen-go, Makizono-cho, Kagoshima-ken 899-65
> PHONE: 0995-77-2114   PRICE: D
> TRANSPORTATION: From Nishi-Kagoshima Station on the Kagoshima Line, take the bus bound for Hayashida Onsen for 70 minutes. Get off at Myoken Onsen and walk for 10 minutes.
> BY CAR: From Route 223, turn east and cross the bridge at the north end of town.

Kurinodake **Onsen**

Up a quiet, steeply winding mountain road, this pretty, friendly inn lies all by itself at the edge of a forest-shrouded *jigokudani* (hell valley). Several such places dot the Japanese landscape, comprising dozens of boiling pools and vents through which sulfuric steam and boiling water escape from subterranean pressures. They make for intriguing walks. Most guests at Nanshukan now stay in the *shinkan*, or new wing, which was completed in

1989. In late 1993, it looked like it had opened yesterday, so meticulous is the maintenance. Our bright room, "Kiri," was a spare but spacious ten tatami mats plus a large, light-wood-floored sitting area and Western-style toilet. The walls were tea-green throughout, accented with light wood and unusual, horizontal-slatted shoji. Dinner, served in a private room, proved refreshingly atypical. It included broiled trout marinated in *miso* paste, a cook-your-own *mazegohan*, an unusual warm *chawanmushi* with a salty plum, *mochi*, steamed chicken, and several side dishes. The chef even took time to stop by for a chat. Nanshukan's four baths, all indoors, are extremely hot. Your best bet is probably to run lots of cold water into the small tub on the first floor of the *shinkan*, churning as you do so. This bath features a nice combination of *hinoki* and tile. All in all, a bargain.

Nanshūkan
6357 Kiba, Kurino-machi, Kagoshima-ken 899-62
PHONE: 0995-74-3511   PRICE: B
TRANSPORTATION: From Kurino Station on the Hikitsu Line, a taxi takes about 15 minutes.

Appendixes

APPENDIX 1
Onsen Pointers

· Bathing Time

Unlike regular inns, *onsen* usually allow twenty-four-hour access to their baths except for the mid-morning hours when some inns are cleaning their tubs. Japanese are pretty predictable about when they bathe. To maximize privacy for you and yours, head for the bath right after dinner. Most Japanese wait an hour or so to let their food digest. Late night is another quiet period, as is the 3 P.M. to 4:30 P.M. time slot.

· Checking In and Out

Since dinner is invariably served between 5:30 and 7 P.M., try to arrive by 4 P.M. so you'll have time for a leisurely bath beforehand. As you enter the inn, you'll be asked to register either at the front desk or in your room. A maid will guide you to your quarters and in most cases serve tea and a sweet. Sometimes she'll sit with you for a while. This is your chance to ask any questions that come to mind. Although it's not always expected, a nice gesture would be to slip her two thousand yen wrapped in tissue paper (while saying "*dozo*") if you discern that she is an employee rather than a member of the manager's family. She initially may refuse but eventually will accept it. This practice in supposedly tip-free Japan can sometimes pay off handsomely. At one inn we visited, everyone else was required to eat in the dining room but our grateful maid served us all our meals in our room. Other than this initial gesture, avoid tipping. Attempting to do so can cause great embarrassment for the employee.

Checkout time is almost always 10 A.M. But you'll probably be awakened by 8 for breakfast, plenty of time for a final bath afterward.

x2∂·¹⁄₀

Most inns in this guide accept only cash, so be prepared. In addition to the per-person rate, you'll usually be charged a small hot-spring levy, a three per cent consumption tax, occasionally a 10–15 percent service charge, and you'll have to pay for whatever beverages you consume. If you want to tarry for a while after checking out, that's rarely a problem. You won't have access to your room but most inns have common areas where you can relax between baths.

· Daytime Dipping

Many of the inns in this guide are near others. Most allow non-staying guests to use their baths for a nominal charge of 200 to 1,000 yen. (Takaragawa's 2,000 yen is confiscatory). Take advantage of these if you have time. Also, some hot springs lack fresh hot water. So if, after a couple of days of visiting *onsen* you want to wash off the accumulated minerals, search out a *kokumin shukusha* or *kyodoburo* for a refreshing rinse. The former is a nationwide chain of modern, economical "people's lodges" and the latter are town-managed "common baths." Both almost always offer hot, freshwater showers—in addition to mineral baths—for a modest charge.

· Etiquette

Foreigners are relatively rare at many of the featured inns, some of which have grown reluctant to accept non-Japanese guests be-cause of their occasional ignorant or boorish behavior. Help pre-serve these treasure spots by blending in as much as possible and refraining from undue demands or excesses. One of the greatest nightmares of *onsen* managers is a foreigner trying to take a Western-style bath, with soap in the water. In Japan, you dowse yourself from buckets or a shower outside the bath, soap down, then rinse off thoroughly before entering the water, which is strictly for soaking. Even if you washed just an hour earlier you should at least splash your privates a few times before entering the bath. Proper etiquette dictates that you not immerse your small towel (see below) in the bath, though some Japanese seem to forget this.

· Hiking

Japan has an abundance of trails, and many of the inns in this book are on or near one. Most have maps showing nearby paths. In some areas it's fairly easy to spend a day or more hiking from *onsen* to *onsen*.

· Meals

Dinner and breakfast are part of the normal package. Depending on the inn, they will be served in your room or in a dining hall (*shokudo*). It's usually difficult to get dinner after 7 P.M. or breakfast after 8:30 A.M. The menus are fixed, although some places offer extra specialties, such as a stew of wild boar or deer, for a premium. You'll also usually be asked by your maid when you arrive what you want to drink with dinner. If you can't start the day without coffee, take a jar of instant. Some places now offer fresh brewed coffee, but this is still rare.

· Mixed Bathing

Once routine, *kon'yoku* has largely disappeared thanks to the postwar influence of American Puritanism. As a rule, the further north in Honshu you go, the more often you'll encounter mixed-sex bathing. At places like Tashiromotoyu, there's no choice at all. Most women find the inn-supplied small towels to be large enough to protect their modesty. Others take along larger bathtowels with which they can wrap themselves. More inns are providing them these days. Wearing a swimsuit is beneath contempt and I've omitted an otherwise worthy inn from this guide for permitting it. "Integrating" an empty men's or women's bath is pretty easy because you can almost always hear or see other bathers arriving at the dressing room. When that happens, simply excuse yourself if you're of the wrong sex.

· Rail & Rent-a-Car

It's hard to beat the freedom of getting around by car, and Japan Railways' rail and rent-a-car program helps make that easy. When you buy the package you get a discount on both your train tickets and a car, which you pick up at the station. If your party is of four or five people, the amount you save on the tickets and the foregone bus or taxi fares can often cover the cost of the car. The option is available from most major stations. You'll need a Japanese or international driver's license.

· Reservations

Most of the inns in this guide are well enough known by Japanese cognoscenti, or are so small, that <u>reservations are a must</u>, especially on weekends. Some of the best places are fully booked for Saturday nights months in advance. Seni, for one, is often booked solid every day for weeks ahead. Putting yourself on a waiting list can sometimes pay off. Unless you speak reasonable Japanese, get an agent or a fluent friend to make your reservation for you by phone. Some inns ask for a deposit, which you can send in cash from a post office by *genkin kakitome*, or cash-registered mail.

· Rules

Like many other Japanese institutions, *onsen* impose lots of regulations, many seemingly arbitrary. Most post signs strictly forbidding drinking and smoking in the baths. These go widely ignored. So do those that ban bringing your own food or drink into the inn. Other rules are more annoying, such as the one at Fukiage in Yamagata that says you can't bathe after 9 A.M. (checkout isn't until 10 A.M.). Kawakami's bizarre schedule for men's and women's use of the *rotenburo* bends the mind. Having to eat breakfast at 7 A.M. or never at some places is downright ridiculous. But if politely requested, some of these rules can be bent. If you can't reach your inn in time for the standard 6 P.M. dinner, for example, call ahead and you'll probably be accommodated.

· Saké in the Bath

Nothing enhances a hot-spring dip more than a cup of rice wine close at hand. Since breakables are a bad idea, I <u>always buy a</u> *kamipakku* (carton) of saké and *purasuchikku koppu* <u>(plastic cups)</u> on the way to the *onsen*. Take them to the bath in a plastic bag and modestly offer drinks around to your fellow bathers. There's no surer path to instant acceptance.

· Self-Cooking (*Jisuibu*)

If you're on a tight budget, consider staying in the *jisuibu* section available at some inns. This is a separate wing for guests staying for at least a few days who prefer to cook their own meals in return for a dramatically reduced price—somewhere in the 2,000–3,000 yen per night range. Cookware, stoves, and refrigerators are provided, and sometimes a grocery shop. In return, you get less privacy and more noise than in the main inn. But besides economizing, your chances of intimate contact with "real" Japanese are greatly enhanced.

· Tipping

See "Checking In and Out" (p. 163).

· Towels

Virtually all inns outside Hokkaido and the most rustic in Tohoku supply a free but skimpy *taoru* (a large handcloth, the thinner type is called a *tenugui*) that's *de rigueur* when you go to the bath. In a pinch you can buy one at the front desk. Use the towel to cover your privates. Purists say you shouldn't take the towel into the water but some Japanese do. Believe it or not, the wrung-out towels actually do a great job of drying you off. Feel free to take them home to use as rags. Some inns provide full-sized bath towels these days, primarily for women to wrap themselves in for mixed bathing. However, the large towels are not for taking home.

· Water Temperature

Many foreigners are convinced that *onsen* water is just too hot. There's no denying that at some places it is. But this rarely needs to be a problem. For one thing, many *onsen* offer several pools that can vary widely in temperature. If one is scalding, try another. Generally speaking, *rotenburo* feel more temperate than indoor baths. In many places you'll see hoses attached to cold-water spigots, or faucets directly over the bath. If it's uncomfortable, run some cold water for a few minutes. Churning the pool to pull cooler water up from the bottom can also help. Finally, the water always feels hottest at first try. Give it ten seconds or so before deciding it's simply intolerable. Also remember that in the hotter baths, proper bathing technique involves several short dips, not one long soak.

· *Yukata*

Virtually all but the most rustic inns provide this light, cotton kimono that most guests wear from arrival till departure, even in the dining room and while strolling around the environs. They're not to be taken away as free souvenirs. If the one in your room is too small, ask for a *dai* (large) or *tokudai* (extra-large) *yukata*. When it's cold, most inns also provide a heavier outer garment called *tanzen* that you wear over the *yukata*.

APPENDIX 2
Mixed Bathing

Kon'yoku, or sexually integrated bathing, is slowly disappearing in Japan. But it's still extant at a surprising number of places. In reference to this guide, you'll find *kon'yoku* available at the following inns (an asterisk indicates *kon'yoku* at the *rotenburo* only):

Hokkaido
Horoka
Meto*
Pirika*
Tokachidake*

Tohoku
Aoni*
Doroyu*
Fudoyu*
Fukiage Hounkaku*
Gaga*
Geto*
Kurokawa*
Magoroku*
Matsukawa Shofuso* (cave bath also)
Namari
Namekawa
Osawa*
Tamagawa

Tashiro Motoyu
Tsurunoyu*
Yunodai
Yunokura*

Kanto
Chuji*
Hatcho no Yu*
Hoshi
Itamuro Daikokuya*
Shionoyu Myogaya*
Yugashima Yumotokan*

Chubu
Akaishi*
Nakabusa
Renge*
Seni (cave bath)
Shirahone Yumoto Saito*
Wayama Jinseikan*

Chugoku
Hannyaji
Sekigane Onseiro*

Kyushu
Akagawa*
Jigoku*
Kurinodake
Yufuin Sanso Yamashige

APPENDIX 3
Hot Spring List

HOKKAIDO

Hot Spring	*Inn*
Daisetsu Kōgen　大雪高原	Daisetsu Kōgen Sansō　大雪高原山荘
Horoka　幌加	Horoka Onsen Ryokan　幌加温泉旅館
Metō　芽登	Metō Onsen　芽登温泉
Pirika　美利河	Yama no Ie　山の家
Sakurano　桜野	Kumanesō　熊嶺荘
Tokachidake　十勝岳	Ryōunkaku　凌雲閣
Yamada　山田	Yamada Onsen Hotel Fukuhara　山田温泉ホテル福原

TOHOKU

Aomori p. 26

Aoni　青荷	Aoni Onsen Ryokan　青荷温泉旅館
Nurukawa　温川	Nurukawa Sansō　温川山荘
Tashiro Motoyu　田代元湯	Yamadakan　山田館
Tsuta　蔦	Tsuta Onsen Ryokan　蔦温泉旅館

Iwate p. 32

Dai　台	Nakajima Ryokan　中嶋旅館
Getō　夏油	Getō Onsen Hotel　夏油温泉ホテル
Matsukawa　松川	Shōfūsō　松楓荘
Namari　鉛	Fujisan Ryokan　藤三旅館
Ōsawa　大沢	Kikusuikan　菊水館
Tōshichi　藤七	Saiunsō　彩雲荘

Hot Spring	Inn

Akita p. 39

Doroyu　泥湯	Okuyama Ryokan　奥山旅館
Kuroyu　黒湯	Kuroyu Onsen　黒湯温泉
Magoroku　孫六	Magoroku Onsen　孫六温泉
Tamagawa　玉川	Tamagawa Onsen　玉川温泉
Tsurunoyu　鶴の湯	Tsurunoyu Onsen　鶴の湯温泉

Miyagi p. 44

Fukiage　吹上	Hōunkaku　峯雲閣
Gaga　戞々	Gaga Onsen　戞々温泉
Yunokura　湯ノ倉	Yueikan　湯栄館

Yamagata p.49

Asahi　朝日	Asahi Onsen Naturalist no Ie　朝日温泉
	ナチュラリストの家
Ginzan　銀山	Notoya Ryokan　能登屋旅館
Namekawa　滑川	Fukushimaya　福島屋
Shirabu　白布	Nishiya Ryokan　西屋旅館
Ubayu　姥湯	Masugataya　桝形屋
Yunodai　湯ノ台	Yumotoya　湯元屋

Fukushima p. 55

Fudōyu　不動湯	Fudōyu Onsen　不動湯温泉
Oku Tsuchiyu　奥土湯	Kawakami Onsen　川上温泉

KANTO

Tochigi p. 60

Hatchō no Yu　八丁ノ湯	Hatchō no Yu　八丁ノ湯
Itamuro　板室	Daikokuya　大黒屋
Ōmaru　大丸	Ōmaru Onsen Ryokan　大丸温泉旅館
Shionoyu　塩ノ湯	Myōgaya Honkan　明賀屋本館

Gunma p. 65

Chūji　忠治	Chūjikan　忠治館

Hot Spring	Inn
Hatonoyu 鳩の湯	Sankyūrō 三鳩楼
Hōshi 法師	Chōjukan 長寿館
Hotaka 武尊	Kaya no Ie 萱の家
Shimonita 下仁田	Seiryūso 清流荘
Takaragawa 宝川	Ōsenkaku 汪泉閣
Yunodaira 湯ノ平	Shōsenkaku 松泉閣

Saitama p. 75

Shibahara 柴原	Yanagiya 柳屋

Kanagawa p.76

Ashinoyu 芦之湯	Matsuzakaya 松坂屋
Sengoku Shimoyu 仙石下湯	Bangakurō 萬岳楼

CHUBU
Niigata p. 80

Echigo Nagano 越後長野	Rankeisō 嵐渓荘
Renge 蓮華	Hakubadake Renge Onsen 白馬岳蓮華温泉
Takanosu 鷹の巣	Kikuya Ryokan 喜久屋旅館

Ishikawa p. 93

Yoshigaura 葭が浦	Ranpu no Yado ランプの宿
Yukawa 湯川	Ryūōkaku 龍王閣

Nagano p. 96

Inagoyu 稲子湯	Inagoyu Ryokan 稲子湯旅館
Jigokudani 地獄谷	Kōrakukan 後楽館
Kamanuma 釜沼	Daikisen 大喜泉
Komanoyu 駒ノ湯	Komanoyu Ryokan 駒ノ湯旅館
Nakabusa 中房	Nakabusa Onsen Ryokan 中房温泉旅館
Seni 仙仁	Iwanoyu 岩の湯
Shirahone 白骨	Motoyu Saitō Ryokan 元湯斎藤旅館
Wayama 和山	Jinseikan 仁成館

Hot Spring	Inn

Toyama p. 109

Kuronagi　黒薙　　　　　　Kuronagi Onsen　黒薙温泉

Ōmaki　大牧　　　　　　　Ōmaki Onsen Kankō Ryokan　大牧温泉
　　　　　　　　　　　　　観光旅館

Gifu p. 113

Doai　渡合　　　　　　　　Doai Onsen　渡合温泉

Fukuchi　福地　　　　　　　Yumoto Chōza　湯元長座

Norimasa　乗政　　　　　　Komeno Ryokan　米野旅館

Yamanashi p. 118

Akaishi　赤石　　　　　　　Akaishi Onsen　赤石温泉

Shizuoka p. 119

Nanadaru　七滝　　　　　　Kajika-an　河鹿庵

Ōsawa　大沢　　　　　　　Ōsawa Onsen Hotel　大沢温泉ホテル

Yugashima　湯が島　　　　　Yumotokan　湯元館

CHUBU

Kyoto p. 126

Mugenkyō　夢絃峡　　　　　Tsurunoya　鶴乃家

Mie p. 128

Arikuji　有久寺　　　　　　Arikujisō　有久寺荘

Nara p. 130

Tōsenji　湯泉地　　　　　　Yadoyu no Sato　やど湯の里

Wakayama p. 132

Yunomine　湯ノ峰　　　　　Azumaya　あづまや

CHUGOKU

Tottori p. 136

Sekigane　関金　　　　　　Onseirō　温清楼

Okayama 138

Hannyaji　般若寺　　　　　Hannyaji Onsen　般若寺温泉

Hot Spring	Inn

Hiroshima p. 140

Yuki　湯来　　　　　　　　Midorisō　みどり荘

KYUSHU

Oita p. 142

Akagawa　赤川　　　　　　Akagawasō　赤川荘

Ukenokuchi　筌ノ口　　　　Onoya　小野屋

Yufuin　由布院　　　　　　Sansō Yamashige　山荘山重

Kumamoto p. 147

Jigoku　地獄　　　　　　　Seifūsō　清風荘

Kurokawa　黒川　　　　　　Sanga Ryokan　山河旅館

Kurokawa　黒川　　　　　　Yamamizuki　山みず木

Manganji　満願寺　　　　　Zuiunsō　瑞雲荘

Tarutama　垂玉　　　　　　Yamaguchi Ryokan　山口旅館

Kagoshima p. 155

Kurinodake　栗野岳　　　　Nanshūkan　南洲館

Myōken　妙見　　　　　　　Gajoen　雅叙苑

Yunotani　湯ノ谷　　　　　Yunotani Sansō　湯ノ谷山荘

Glossary

aji: horse mackerel, usually dried when served for breakfast at a
    Japanese inn
ayu: a small river fish unique to Japan and with no accepted English
    name. Staple fare at mountain *onsen*

bekkan: annex. Literally "separate wing" but sometimes called *shinkan*,
    or "new wing"

chawanmushi: an egg custard containing *shiitake* mushrooms, chicken,
    ginkgo nuts, a piece of fish cake, and a sprig of something
    green

daiyokujō: main bath. Used chiefly by men
datsuijo: changing room, just outside the bath

enoki: thin-stemmed, sweet mushrooms, often steamed in butter, or
    added to *miso* soup
enkaijō: banquet room

fusuma: the sliding doors or partitions that separate traditional
    Japanese rooms

genkan: main entrance
geta: wooden clogs, usually provided for guests to use when walking
    around the outside of an *onsen* inn

hanare: a cottage set apart from the main building of an inn *himemasu*: brown trout

hinoki: cypress. Sometimes called *hiba*. Japan's most treasured wood. Aromatic and costly, almost all wooden baths are made from it

honkan: main building

inoshishi: wild boar. Although normally domesticated as livestock, the meat is still considered a prized delicacy

irori: traditional indoor charcoal hearth for cooking, heating tea water and getting warm

iwaburo: bath made out of a rock formation, natural or constructed

jingisukan ryôri: Mongolian-style beef or mutton barbeque

jisuibu: section of an inn—often a separate building—for guests who want to cook their own meals (See "Self-Cooking" in Appendix 1, p. 166)

kazokuburo: family bath. Private, cozy, and mainly for couples

kokumin shukusha: literally "citizen's shelters," these large inns provide economical, though rather mundane lodging for budget-minded travelers. Usually located in prime tourist spots, they're convenient for a drop-in shower and shampoo

kon'yoku: mixed bathing, where men and women bathe together in the same pool or spring.

kôsen: a mineral spring that isn't naturally warm or is too tepid for comfortable bathing, and so is artificially heated. In general, *kosen* inns tend to be more rustic, and their baths more utilitarian, than their hotter *onsen* cousins.

kotatsu: popular in old houses without central heating. The traditional *kotatsu* is a wooden frame with a quilt on it, placed over a heater or brazier. Warm your legs by putting them under the quilt

kotsuzake: a hearty drink made by pouring hot saké over river fish (usually char), and served with the fish in a bowl

kyôdôburo: a public or community bathhouse or *onsen*. Occasionally there is a modest charge

mazegohan: rice boiled with various vegetables and seasonings *minshuku*: a guest house, more like a private home that allows boarders. Accommodations are generally more modest, and offered at a lower price, than those at full-scale Japanese inns

miso: a fermented soy bean paste that can be made into soup and used for cooking a variety of dishes. It is a staple of the Japanese diet

nabe: a stew that can include wild boar, duck, seafood, carp, venison, beef or pheasant along with various vegetables. Usually cooked in a small pot at your table

oden: a mixture of meat, fish, and vegetable snacks served in broth. Most popular in the autumn and winter

ofuro: generic term for a bath or hot tub

okami: proprietress, or landlady, usually the owner's wife, daughter, or daughter-in-law. In polite form, *okamisan*

onnaburo: women's bath

onsen-gō: a small district of discrete spas

otokoburo: men's bath

reisen: mineral spring reputed to possess mystical healing powers

rōka: the narrow wooden corridor between the shoji of your room and the windows. Part of it is often used as a sitting area

rotenburo: outdoor bath (a *han-rotenburo* is one that's at least partly roofed)

ryokan: a traditional Japanese inn, usually run by a family

sansai: edible wild plants

sashimi: sliced raw fish served with soy sauce and horseradish

senmenjo: common area with sinks for shaving, tooth-brushing, etc

shabu-shabu: name of a dish eaten by dipping sliced meats and vegetables into a pot of boiling soup on the table

shōchū: traditional distilled spirits, similar to vodka

shokudō: dining room

sunakku: a tiny bar that serves snacks and usually offers *karaoke*

soba: thin buckwheat noodles, eaten cold or served in broth

sudomari: overnight stay without meals

takiyu: a stream of hot water falling from a suspended pipe. The original shower-massage. Sometimes called *utaseyu*, mainly in western Japan

taoru: towel. Here it refers to the skimpy towel wrapped in plastic that you find in your room. A thinner version, called a *tenugui*, in plain cotton is occasionally offered

tororo: grated Japanese yam

uchiburo or *uchiyu*: indoor bath

umecha: tea made from Japanese apricots

uni: sea urchin

yamame: river trout

yukata: the light cotton kimono in your room's closet. In winter there will also be a heavier outer garment called a *tanzen*

yunohana: bits of sulfur and other particulates that occur naturally in some *onsen* water. These can be rather large and grotesque-looking but *yunohana* are not at all a sign that the *onsen* is dirty or contaminated. Connoisseurs welcome them

yuzu: citron, or Chinese lemon

yu-zukare: the fatigue or lassitude resulting from too much bathing

zabuton: cushions used for sitting on the floor of a tatami room